WRITERS AND THEIR WOF

ISOBEL ARMSTRONG
General Editor

BRYAN LOUGHREY
Advisory Editor

Peter Ackroyd

Roderick Field

PETER ACKROYD

Peter Ackroyd

Susana Onega

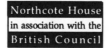

Northcote House
in association with the
British Council

© Copyright 1998 by Susana Onega

First published in 1998 by Northcote House Publishers Ltd, Plymbridge House,
Estover Road, Plymouth PL6 7PY, United Kingdom.
Tel: +44 (01752) 202368 Fax: +44 (01752) 202330.

British Library Cataloguing-in-Publication Data
A catalogue record for this book is available from the British Library

ISBN 0-7463-0839-6

Typeset by PDQ Typesetting, Newcastle-under-Lyme
Printed and bound in the United Kingdom

For my students past, present and future, whose love of literature and desire to learn have provided the stimulus for the writing of this book.

Contents

Acknowledgements

The author acknowledges with thanks Peter Ackroyd's generous assistance and patient co-operation in the preparation of this study. She is also grateful to Isobel Armstrong, who suggested the topic, to Stan Smith, for his specialized advice on the poetry, to Tim Bozman and José Angel García Landa who read the chapters on prose, to the Northcote House copy-editor, Joanna Jellinek, for a most efficient job, to Brian Hulme of Northcote House for his availability and resourcefulness, and to Celestino Deleyto, Constanza del Río, Francisco Collado, María Dolores Herrero, Marita Nadal and Isabel Santaolalla, who undertook to teach her classes *gratis et amore* during her first sabbatical leave in twenty years. Acknowledgements are also due to the publishers of his work for permission to reproduce copyright material, and to the photographer Roderick Field.

This study is part of a research project financed by the Spanish Ministry of Education (PS. 94–0057). The author acknowledges the giving of two travelling grants by the Obra Social y Cultural de la Caja de Ahorros de la Inmaculada (Programa Europa).

Biographical Outline

1949	Born in West London.
1960–67	St Benedict's School, Ealing.
1968–71	Clare College, Cambridge (MA). Graduates with a 'Double First' in English.
1971	Publishes first poetry collection, *Ouch*.
1971–73	Yale University (Mellon Fellow). Writes first critical book, *Notes for a New Culture*, published in 1976.
1973	Publishes second poetry collection, *London Lickpenny*.
1973–77	Literary Editor of the *Spectator*.
1978–81	Jt. Managing Editor of the *Spectator*. Publishes *Country Life* (1978); *Dressing Up: Transvestism and Drag, the History of an Obsession* (1979); first biography, *Ezra Pound and his World* (1980); and first novel, *The Great Fire of London* (1982).
1984	Fellow of the Royal Society of Literature. *The Last Testament of Oscar Wilde* wins Somerset Maugham Prize. *T. S. Eliot* wins Whitbread Prize and Heinemann Award.
1985	*Hawksmoor* wins Whitbread Prize and Guardian Fiction Prize.
1986	Chief book reviewer for *The Times*.
1987	Publishes *The Diversions of Purley* and *Chatterton* shortlisted for the Booker Prize.
1989	Publishes *First Light*.
1990	Publishes *Dickens*. Elected 'Author of the Year' by the English Association of Bookshops.
1991	Publishes *Introduction to Dickens*.
1992	Publishes *English Music*.
1993	Publishes *The House of Doctor Dee*.

1994	Publishes *Dan Leno and the Limehouse Golem*.
1995	Publishes fourth biography, *Blake*.
1996	Publishes ninth novel, *Milton in America*.
1998	Publishes fifth biography, *The Life of Thomas More*.

Abbreviations and References

B.	*Blake* (London: Sinclair-Stevenson, 1995)
C.	*Chatterton* (London: Abacus, 1988)
CL	*Country Life* (London: Ferry Press, 1978)
D.	*Dickens* (London: Sinclair-Stevenson, 1990)
DLLG	*Dan Leno and the Limehouse Golem* (London: Sinclair-Stevenson, 1994)
DP	*The Diversions of Purley and Other Poems* (London: Abacus, 1990)
DU	*Dressing Up: Transvestism and Drag, the History of an Obsession* (London: Thames & Hudson, 1979)
EM	*English Music* (London: Hamish Hamilton, 1992)
EPW	*Ezra Pound and his World* (London: Thames & Hudson, 1980)
FL	*First Light* (London: Abacus, 1990)
GFL	*The Great Fire of London* (London: Abacus, 1984)
H.	*Hawksmoor* (London: Abacus, 1987)
HDD	*The House of Doctor Dee* (London: Hamish Hamilton, 1993)
ID	*Introduction to Dickens* (London: Sinclair-Stevenson, 1991)
LL	*London Lickpenny* (London: Ferry Press, 1973)
LTM	*The Life of Thomas More* (London: Chatto and Windus, 1998)
LTOW	*The Last Testament of Oscar Wilde* (London: Abacus, 1984)
MA	*Milton in America* (London: Sinclair-Stevenson, 1996)
NNC	*Notes for a New Culture* (London: Alkin Books, 1993)
O.	*Ouch* (London: The Curiously Strong Press, 1971)
TSE	*T. S. Eliot* (London: Cardinal, 1989)

1

Only Connect...

Like many a young creative writer, Peter Ackroyd's earliest ventures were in the field of poetry. As he himself has explained, when he was a boy the only thing that interested him was poetry: 'When I was a school boy I wrote poetry. And when I was a student I wrote poetry, and when I was at University or at school all I really wanted to read was poetry. That was my great ambition, to be a poet'.[1] As a Cambridge undergraduate Ackroyd soon showed an extraordinary intellectual curiosity – what he described in *Notes for a New Culture* as 'the intellectual equivalent of bulimia' (*NNC* 7) – that got him a first-class Honours degree in English. As John Walsh has pointed out: 'At Cambridge, his study technique was to immerse himself in every word written by or about an author who interested him, then distil from his reading a single essay of such nitric brilliance that his tutors and examiners could merely swallow hard and wonder about the safety of their tenure.'[2] Moreover, Walsh maintains, Ackroyd would soon show a similar overall acquisitiveness in his writing of novels and biographies.

At Cambridge Ackroyd not only read omnivorously, he also became acquainted with a group of teachers and students, including J. H. Prynne, Andrew Crozier, Ian Patterson and Kevin Strutford, some of whom were actively involved in the revitalization of English poetry along the cosmopolitan and heavily experimental lines set by John Ashbery and the New York School of poetry.

Ackroyd's earliest published poem, 'The Goldfish Sonata', appeared in the March 1971 issue of *The Curiously Strong*,[3] a university poetry journal founded at Cambridge in 1969 by Fred Buck and Ian Patterson in order to promote this new kind of experimental poetry. The six-page issue where Ackroyd placed

'The Goldfish Sonata' also contained poems by Monk Tamming, Ian Patterson, David Rosenberg and Barry Macsweeney. The first issue consisted of two folio sheets printed both sides. It was distributed by post, for just the price of the stamps, to a growing number of sympathizers and soon increased its number of pages and frequency of appearance until it developed into a quarterly with one editor based in London (Fred Buck and later Ian Patterson) and another in New York (Chan and Paul Dorn). It survived until the retirement of Ian Patterson, in 1975, to whom the final issue was dedicated (vol. iv, nos. 9 and 10).

Ackroyd's first poetry collection, *Ouch* (1971), was likewise published in *The Curiously Strong*, in a volume (vol. iv, no. 2) wholly devoted to him. The collection, written just before *Notes for a New Culture*, consisted of fourteen new poems and 'The Goldfish Sonata'. It was edited by Ian Patterson while Ackroyd was at Yale. After *Ouch* Ackroyd published *London Lickpenny* (1973) and *Country Life* (1978) with the Ferry Press, the same press that was publishing the poetry of J. H. Prynne, a lecturer in English at Cambridge and one of the most rebarbative avant-garde English poets. In fact, Prynne and Ashbery are the two poets Ackroyd acknowledges as his most influential predecessors.[4] Most of Ackroyd's poems in these three collections, currently out of print, are available in *The Diversions of Purley* (1987), where they have been reprinted with a few new poems, arranged in an apparently casual, faintly thematic order. Two poems from *Country Life* ('There are so many' and 'the novel', reprinted as 'on any kind of novel') and 'The great Sun', also reprinted in *The Diversions of Purley*, were first published in the *Partisan Review*,[5] as part of a selection of 'New English Poets' made by John Ashbery who was at that time the poetry editor of the journal. Besides Ackroyd, Ashbery's list of new poets included Deborah Evans, Alan Fuchs, Lee Harwood, Anthony Howell, Iliassa Sequin, Fiona Templeton and John Welch.

After Cambridge Peter Ackroyd was granted a Mellon fellowship that enabled him to spend two years at Yale University. During his stay at Yale he wrote *Notes for a New Culture*, a book of criticism we can consider Ackroyd's early poetic manifesto, as it casts significant light on Ackroyd's own poetic as well as fictional practice. In it Ackroyd tries to systematize his own response to contemporary English culture and to formulate the

2

basic tenets of his own attitude to literature. As he explains in the Preface to the revised edition, 'if anyone were foolish enough to study all of my later books in sequence – the biographies as well as the novels and the volumes of poetry – I believe that the concerns, or obsessions, of *Notes for a New Culture* would be found in more elaborate form within them' (*NNC* 8).

As Peter Conrad has pointed out, the title of Ackroyd's book echoes T. S. Eliot's *Notes Towards the Definition of Culture* (1948). Conrad explains, 'Eliot, with characteristic irony gave a hesitant, deferential title to his essay [although his] notes are not at all extemporary or provisional: they comprise a sermon'.[6] By contrast, Ackroyd's notes 'are not papal bulls but a series of dangerous missiles [...] designed to irritate his readers into reconsidering received opinions'.[7] With Eliot's essay in mind, therefore, and already showing his characteristic magpie acquisitiveness, Ackroyd sets out to trace the evolution of English culture from the Restoration until the twentieth century, comparing it to the different development taking place in Europe during the same period. His main argument is that contemporary English culture is a declining culture (*NNC* 11), because it has been incapable of keeping pace with the most innovative – or 'modernist' – developments elsewhere, due to what he considers to be a backward attachment to humanist values.

Ackroyd points to a basic dichotomy between what he calls the 'modernist' and the 'humanist' cultural outlooks, character-ized in terms of their respective attitudes to self, world and language. His main contention is that while for the 'humanists' language remains transparent, a mere tool for the expression of human values and human nature, that is, an aesthetic instrument for the communication of the experience of the moral self, for the 'modernists' language is an autonomous entity, a self-begetting universe of discourse without referent or content. According to Ackroyd, aesthetic humanism reaches its peak in the 1930s and 1940s in the work of New Critics like F. R. Leavis, John Crowe Ransom and Cleanth Brooks, who define literature in aesthetic and moral terms as the linguistic expression of man, and criticism simply as the study of style. Aesthetic humanism informs the literature written by Georgian and Edwardian writers who postulate the morality and utilitarian nature of art such as John

3

Galsworthy, Leslie Stephen and G. E. Moore, and is continued in the 1950s by Movement writers like Philip Larkin, Kingsley Amis and John Wain.

The most important arguments against this theoretical position are raised by modernist writers like James Joyce and Alain Robbe-Grillet and by critics like Roland Barthes and Jacques Derrida. For such writers, aesthetic humanism is based on a false notion of the human 'individual' – or subject – as a constant or identifiable essence or 'self'. In fact, they contend, the subject is better described as a process, an interaction of material, historical, social and psychological factors, each of which is in its turn determined by and forms part of numerous other processes. Likewise, where for the 'humanists' language has a utilitarian function, for the 'modernists' it becomes a self-sufficient and autonomous sign-system without meaning or referent. Taking writing – as opposed to speech – as the original linguistic form, Barthes substitutes the notion of 'text' for that of literary genres and defines criticism as the 'metalanguage of literature', and literature itself as 'the science of language' (NNC 115) . As Ackroyd further explains, this 'modernist' redefinition of 'self' and 'text' finds expression in the poetry of Cambridge School writers like J. H. Prynne and Andrew Crozier, and of New York School poets like Frank O'Hara and John Ashbery. And (we may add), it also informs his own poetry.

Early reviewers of Notes for a New Culture held contradictory opinions. Peter Conrad, for example, welcomes Ackroyd's attempt to disclose 'an underground tradition of artists whose virtue is not the ponderous centrality Leavis acclaims but their ironic marginal status as 'conspirators and snipers' and concludes that the book is 'quarrelsome, acute, bracing and should be read'.[8] Other reviewers, however, have regarded the stark dichotomy between 'humanism' and 'modernism' as too schematic and sweeping. David Lodge, for example, underlined the book's stylistic obscurity – which he considered to be a conscious rhetorical device, the result of Ackroyd's alignment with modernism – and condemned what he described as 'the curious distortions and oversimplifications of Mr Ackroyd's cultural history'.[9] Avowedly, Ackroyd's decision to use the term 'modernist' diachronically, including under the same label such disparate cultural, literary and philosophical phenomena as

4

Enlightenment poetics, high modernist literature, pop art, German phenomenology, post-Saussurean linguistics, Lacanian psychoanalysis, the diverse poststructuralisms, and Derridean deconstruction may be confusing and even misleading, above all if *Notes for a New Culture* is to be read as a comprehensive critical assessment of the parallel yet divergent evolutions of English and European cultures from the late seventeenth century to the present era. Peter Ackroyd himself is now ready to admit that the book was probably conditioned by the 'impatience of youth and the fact that I was only interested in poetry, and English poetry had during those decades of my lifetime gone through a very steep decline in interest as far as I was concerned'.[10] Still, the book can be quite useful if read as Ackroyd's most sustained theoretical statement of his own ideas about the English literary tradition, at the crucial moment when he has trying to formulate his own definition of literature and to find his own vital answers to the questions about self, world and text which were soon to inform his own poetry and prose fiction.

Throughout the book Ackroyd shows his contempt for 'aesthetic humanism' and his admiration and respect for such modernist writers as Joyce, Robbe-Grillet, Prynne and Ashbery, who sought 'a new kind of freedom' by suggesting the 'ability of literature to explore the problems and ambiguities of a *formal absolute* which will never be experience. [Even though these new literary] forms seem to proclaim the death of Man' (*NNC* 149, my emphasis). In other words, *Notes for a New Culture* helps us situate Ackroyd within the anti-realist, cosmopolitan and experimental poetic trend that was emerging at the University of Cambridge while he was there as a student, as a reaction against humanism in general and against the Movement in particular, the mainstream British trend of the fifties and sixties, represented by writers such as Philip Larkin, John Wain, Kingsley Amis, Robert Conquest, D. J. Enright, John Holloway and Elizabeth Jennings. Originally launched by D. J. Scott, the literary editor of the *Spectator*, in an anonymous leading article entitled 'In the Movement' (1 October 1954), as a way of increasing the sales, the Movement quickly came to represent the aims and attitudes of the new post-Second World War, welfare state generation. As Blake Morrison[11] has explained, the origins of the Movement go back to Oxford in the early 1940s,

5

when a number of key friendships were made. The first and most important was that between Larkin and Amis, followed a little later by that between Bruce Montgomery and John Wain. Described as a provincial, lower-middle class generation of scholarship-winning, Oxbridge educated university teachers, the members of the Movement were characterized by militant anti-romanticism, anti-experimentalism and anti-cosmopolitanism, summarized in their deeply felt distaste for Dylan Thomas, the epigone of everything they found objectionable, ugly and immoral in the field of poetry. Deeply influenced by the logical positivist school of philosophy of which A. J. Ayer's *Language, Truth and Logic* (1936) was the first exposition in the English language, Movement writers considered themselves realists and empiricists; they defended the transparent and utilitarian use of language and contended that the vast majority of utterances produced by poets do have literal, paraphrasable meaning.

The university circle at Cambridge where Ackroyd found himself between 1968 and 1971 was geared by the desire to overturn this kind of neorealist – or humanist, in Ackroyd's terms – poetry along the modernist lines described in *Notes for a New Culture*, that is, by the radical redefinition of language and of self and world. As Ackroyd explains in *Notes for a New Culture*, in the poetry of Movement writes like Philip Larkin, as well as in that of younger poets like Sylvia Plath and Ted Hughes: 'Everything is mediated through a single level of language that transforms even apparently subtle statements into a dense and simplistic language of private experience' (*NNC* 127). Modernist poets like Prynne, Ashbery and O'Hara, by contrast, manage to create a unique space for the experience of subjectivity by shifting the emphasis from the fixed or central perspective of the lyrical 'I' to the procedure of the poem itself.

In the kind of experimental poetry Ackroyd admires, the refusal to acknowledge the existence of any consistent or identifiable notion of subject is often expressed by means of baffling slips and shifts of viewpoint, the change of direction in mid-sentence and the resistance to giving a poem any identifiable perspective. Likewise, as self and word recede into the background or simply disappear, the poetry becomes poetry '"about language" and nothing else'.[12] In other words, the poetry turns into 'language poetry' as opposed to the 'poetry of things', a poetry written on the assumption that poetry should not have the simple communicative function of everyday language, that it should not have any commonsensical or paraphrasable meaning, but rather work to illuminate itself. As Ackroyd explains in *Notes for a New Culture*, the refusal to accept the traditional notions of autonomous subject and transparent language inevitably leads to the proposition that poetry is arbitrary and fictional: 'Since there is nothing to be "said" everything can be included; and since at the centre of the language is the active process of the poem itself, every external reference and object lies somewhere on the periphery. And this includes most of all, the ubiquitous and apparent "I"' (*NNC* 29). To put it differently, once we accept the Derridean contention that language is perpetually distant from its origin, that the signs of language refer only to other signs and texts to other texts, literature becomes *le jeu de la forme*, the free play of linguistic forms without origins (*NNC* 144).

Ackroyd's poetry is fully in line with this type of arbitrary and fictional 'language poetry', as can be seen, for example, from a simple reading of the poems' titles. In the 'poetry of things' the title is often used to summarize the poem's content. By contrast, in the few cases in which Ackroyd's poems do have a title, we find that they obscure, rather than illuminate, the meaning. 'The Goldfish Sonata', for example is a title so little related to the poem itself that we lose nothing when Ackroyd decides to reprint it in *London Lickpenny* as 'The Island Sonata', for indeed the poem is neither about goldfish nor islands. That is to say, Ackroyd has chosen a totally unrelated and absurd title for his poem, similar to that of Eugène Ionesco's *The Bald Prima Donna*, an absurdist play which has nothing to do either with baldness or with opera singers. Other times, title and poem are ironically opposed, as happens, for example, with 'Country Life', the poem that gives the second collection its title. As the first sentence of the poem already makes clear ('The streets of the great city when they are empty') the poem – and the whole collection as well – deals with the alienation of life in the city. It is a prose sketch containing the dream of a patient called Jeremy, and the parodic analysis of the dream by his psycho-analyst, who gets entangled in a pseudo-scientific attempt to dissect the dream into a meaningful, logical pattern.

7

On other occasions Ackroyd changes the original title of a poem when reprinting it, in order to make it even more opaque. For example, there is a poem in *Ouch* entitled 'Scenes from Modern Life', that is reprinted in *London Lickpenny* as 'Prose Poem' and in *The Diversions of Purley* as 'A Prose Poem'. That is to say, Ackroyd substitutes the earlier title that referred to the poem's subject matter by another that simply describes its form, and then adds the indefinite article to the *London Lickpenny* version, thus increasing its imprecision: the title does not refer any longer to a particular prose poem, but just to *a* poem in prose.

The willed unrelatedness and opacity of such titles is a growing feature in Ackroyd's poetry as a whole, a fact obscured, however, by another disorienting technique: the rearrangement of the earlier with the later poems in the successive reprints. Reading the poems in the order in which they were first published, it is possible to see an increasing reluctance to give significant titles to the poems, to the point that most of the poems in *The Diversions of Purley* do not even have a title, but are simply named after their first line, a common practice at the end of the nineteenth century and one which was used by W. H. Auden in the 1930s and also sometimes by Laura Riding; it suggests a lack of interest on the part of the poet to indicate a clear subject matter. More significantly, poems that originally had a title sometimes lose it when reprinted, as happens, for example, to a poem entitled 'Romance' in *London Lickpenny*, that is named in *The Diversions of Purley* simply after the first two words in the first line: 'and then...' In this sense it might be interesting to point out that virtually the only changes Ackroyd has made in the reprinted versions of his earlier poems are precisely title changes or title erasures such as these.

Another traditional function of titles in the 'poetry of things' is to allude to a particular generic tradition or thematic convention, thus creating a specific horizon of expectations for the reader. This function is parodied by Ackroyd, whose titles often allude to a tradition or convention ironically. An example of this would be 'Among School Children', first published in *Ouch* and reprinted in *London Lickpenny* and *The Diversions of Purley*. The title has been borrowed from W. B. Yeats's well-known poem in *The Tower*. In Yeats's poem, a 60-year-old teacher muses on the classical topos of time as destroyer of beauty as he

8

compares the 'kind old nun in white hood' with the children in the classroom ('I look upon one child or th'other there/ And wonder if she stood so at that age'[13]). So the title situates Ackroyd's poem in the shadow of the great master and within a well-known genre. The horizon of expectations thus raised is, however, flaunted by the poem when the lyrical 'I' unemotionally concedes that his wildly romantic utterances might be just a way of earning his living ('my terrific love-cries/ are probably for sale'), and that the only response they are likely to produce is a dismissive commentary by a critic in a specialized journal ('the technician said, "these poems are a wounded/ fawn"'). In the second stanza the narrator's vital experiences about love, his position in the universe, and in society ('(a) love-cries/ (b) quantum (c) unemployed') are likewise deprived of meaning by the schoolteacher's unemotional request for the children to reduce them to a paraphrasable formula: 'Try to explain in your own words how/ the writer felt when he saw the girl/ with eyes like broken glass'. The schoolteacher's proposal to analyse the poem brings to mind Wordsworth's impatient rejection of reason in 'The Tables Turned': 'Our meddling intellect/ Misshapes the beauteous forms of things:/ We murder to dissect'.[14] But Ackroyd's appropriation of Yeats's and Wordsworth's poems is further complicated by allusion. Mixed up with the Yeatsian and Wordsworthian echoes we also find an implausible pastiche of T. S. Eliot's 'The Hollow Men' in one of the sentences to be analysed by the children that is repeated twice by the schoolteacher: 'your eyes are like broken glass'. As the reader of Eliot cannot help realizing, this sentence combines 'the broken glass' of the 'dry cellar' where the hollow men live, and 'The eyes' of the just that are 'Sunlight on a broken column'.[15] The children, however, are not analysing Eliot's poem, but a poem by the speaker that includes Eliot's lines.

This and the other questions asked by the teacher ('What do these words mean...?', 'Have you ever met anyone with eyes like broken glass?'...'If not, would you like to?') are never answered. In other words, Ackroyd has built a poem about the futility of the poet's task on the sheer accumulation and incongruous combination of romantic and anti-romantic allusions to three key poets in the English canon, but the reader is not sure about the relationship established between

9

the poem and the literary traditions thus alluded to. It is neither a new version, nor a parodic transformation of a classical topic, as the title had led us to expect, but simply a self-conscious and imitative linguistic palimpsest, whose only meaning is to suggest the free play of language and meaning. However, for all its derivative character, the reader cannot help but feel the strength of the poem itself, the fact that Ackroyd's poem is a real poem indeed, paradoxically built as it is on the accumulation of intertextual echoes. As we shall see, Ackroyd goes on to use the same technique in the writing of his novels.

A key contention of the New Criticism, summarized in Cleanth Brooks's *The Well-Wrought Urn*, is that every poem is a complete, autonomous whole, whose form and content are inextricably united in order to create an internal structure of meaning. Many of Ackroyd's poems seem to have been written to demonstrate the futility of this contention. Some poems, such as 'The first axiom...' (*LL*), for example, may be described as virtuoso displays of linguistic form without paraphrasable content.

> The first axiom of this proposition is that the firppppppppppppp
> the the the the the the the the the the
> spanish fly, my own true
> tttttttttoooppppppppppppoopopopopopopopo
> by the banks of the Iffey I
> ooooooooooooooooooooooooooh
> and so to bed, and so to bed, and so to bed, and so to bed
> ouch
> whatisthislifeiffullofcarewehavenotimeto
> the supreme penalty
> is   is   is   is

In this 'language poem', letters, phrases and words chosen at random from the Borgesian Library of Babel coexist with each other and repeat themselves in an apparently haphazard way, directing the reader's attention to the materiality of the linguistic signs themselves. However, for all its awkwardness, the line 'whatisthislifeiffullofcarewehavenotimeto' can be recognized as a reproduction of the first two lines of 'Leisure', the best-known poem of the 'tramp poet', W. H. Davies ('What is this life if, full of care,/ We have no time to stand and stare'.[16] Significantly, the lines thus incorporated have been smashed

10

together and left unfinished, in an attempt to deprive them of denotative as well as connotative signification, thus reducing them to their materiality.

Another example of a poem aimed at producing a purely visual impact would be 'the poem' (CL). It is made up of thematically unrelated words and phrases apparently scattered on the page in an arbitrary way. Such poems bring to mind the concrete poems of Guillaume Apollinaire, whose *Calligrammes* (1918) announced the development of symbolist poetry towards surrealism. However, Apollinaire's formal experimentation, in poems such as 'La bouteille', where the poem has the form of a bottle, were aimed at enhancing the inseparability and complementarity of form and content, whereas in these poems by Ackroyd form is rather meant to underline the emptiness of the linguistic patterns and the arbitrariness of their arrangement on the blank page.

In other cases, Ackroyd uses more traditional stanzaic forms for the same purpose. For example, Ackroyd's first published poem, 'The Goldfish Sonata', consists of four stanzas made up of eight lines of variable length without consistent rhyme, but carefully arranged with different degrees of indentation that suggest a complex formal structure. However, as a reading of the poem would make clear, its form is devoid of significance *vis à vis* the poem's conceivable content or meaning, which is, simply stated, unparaphrasable. The first stanza runs as follows:

> was she in the arms of sunlight
> wheelchairs pass
> & public safety passes
> one bankrupt glance:
> she fades like tap-water
> oh the vanity of human lipstick!
> or, who sucks what mister
> or, let museums dream you my dear

Formally, the stanza seems to have been planned on the transgression of the most basic rules of traditional poetry: the absence of consistent end-line rhymes contrasts with the elaborate indentation at the beginning of each line, the anaphoric repetition of 'or' at the beginning of the last two lines – underlined by the visual anaphoric effect of 'one' and 'oh' at the beginning of lines 4 and 6 – and the alliteration or

11

cross alliteration of 'w' ('was'/'wheelchair'; 'who'/'what'), of 'p' ('pass'/'public'/'passes'), and of 'm' ('mister'/'museum') give the stanza a formal aspect that is, however, undermined by the repetition of the same verb ('pass' and 'passes') on lines 2 and 3; by the parodic use of traditional poetic devices, like the opening of the poem with a rhetorical question ('was she in the arms of sunlight'); and the use of admirations ('oh the vanity of human lipstick!'), for no particular reason at all, since the expectations raised by these two lines – that we are reading a lyrical poem about a woman in the tradition of high romanticism – are never fulfilled in the rest of the poem. Indeed, as a reading of the first stanza already makes clear, the whole poem has been constructed as a collage, through the juxtaposition of sentences whose meaning is totally unrelated to each other and whose registers are discordant. The stale romantic flavour of lines 1 and 6, for example, may be described as red herrings, that is, allusions that lead nowhere. They are bathetically undermined in the lines following them, which are thematically incongruous and stylistically belong to more prosaic and crude linguistic registers.

Such bathetic juxtapositions of incompatible styles and red herring allusions are combined in this stanza with two other features that are characteristic of Ackroyd's poetry in general. One is the use of incongruous or aborted similes, as for example, in 'she fades like tap-water' in line 5, or 'secrets continue like the radio' in line 4 of the second stanza, and the other, the coining of opaque metaphors, like 'the nation's unemployed/ lying tomahawked in rice', in the first two lines of the fourth stanza. Where the difficulty of understanding metaphors in the traditional 'poetry of things' would depend on implicit logical connections between the two terms of the comparison, or at least on the reader's capacity to guess the subjective relationships between them, in a construction such as this there is no expectation of any logical or subjective meaning: 'the nation's unemployed/ lying tomahawked in rice' can only arbitrarily be said to suggest the meagre condition of the English unemployed, for the connotations of 'tomahawked' and 'rice' confuse rather than throw light on the suggested meaning as they send the perplexed reader's association of ideas in totally unrelated, arbitrary directions. In other words, where even the wildest and most personal metaphoric or symbolic constructions in the

12

'poetry of things' might be said to be based on some kind of logic, the meaning of Ackroyd's metaphor hesitates between two equally absurd sets of connotations, offering itself as an arbitrary concatenation of self-referential signifiers, expressing only the autonomy and self-sufficiency of language.

In 'The Goldfish Sonata', therefore, we already find the most important features Ackroyd will recurrently use in his later poetry. It is an 'empty' poetry, as opposed to the traditional 'poetry of things', a poetry about language, from which the notions of 'self' and 'world' have been totally erased, a poetry written solely to express that basic tenet of the New York School, that, in John Ashbery's words, 'understanding comes about . . . as a sort of Penelope's web that's constantly being taken apart when it's almost completed, and that's the way we grow in our knowledge, and experience'.[17]

As we have seen in the above examples, Peter Ackroyd strives hard to continue writing this kind of empty 'language poetry' in his later collections. However, a simple comparison of 'The Goldfish Sonata' with the first poem in *Ouch*, 'The hermaphrodite suffers a change' would already reveal an interesting tension between theory and practice. The title of the poem is simply its first line, but the title is related to the poem's content and, in contrast to 'The Goldfish Sonata', the poem *does* have paraphrasable meaning: 'The hermaphrodite suffers a change' indeed is a poem about a crucial moment in the life of a young gay. What is more, for all the attempts at hiding it, we can clearly hear the voice of the lyrical 'I', struggling to make itself heard. In fact, the struggle to suffocate the voice of the speaker and to divest the poem of personal or emotive content creates a characteristic tension:

the hermaphrodite suffers a change; now he is alone
& the surface is wonderful, he sits in the silence
of trains, he just reads old magazines

you have reached the desert station, & your perfect
friends are out of place; their ironies make your
heart thump

on looking onto the world, your eyes got bloodshot;
the Poet wears violet shades, he is freaming [*scilicet* dreaming] of things
to come. Alas his art is dead.

While in 'The Goldfish Sonata' the reader could not find any kind of consistent narrative voice or point of view, in this new poem the narrative voice is clearly there, although concealed under different disguises: the poem is about 'the hermaphrodite', addressed as 'you' by the narrator. However, as the equation of 'the hermaphrodite' to 'the Poet' in the third stanza makes clear, 'the Poet' and 'the hermaphrodite' are one and the same. What appeared at first sight as the detached external narrator's description of the hermaphrodite's feelings are now revealed as the self-addressed and interiorized musings of 'the Poet'. What is more, in a further development, the identity of 'the Poet' is eventually hinted at in the sixth stanza, where a homosexual chance encounter, heightened to the category of 'love without end', is defiantly set against the 'sexual practices' that 'decorate the wonderful smile of his father', possibly a reference to Ackroyd's own father, the painter Graham Ackroyd, who separated Ackroyd from his mother shortly after his birth. The tension created between Ackroyd's conscious attempt to hide the central perspective of the lyrical 'I' and his unconscious desire to reveal it and to affirm the uniqueness of his own poetic voice is revealed in the abrupt use of physical crudity that comes as a surprise in the last two stanzas and contrasts with the rest of the poem.

As in 'The Goldfish Sonata', the use of exclamation marks, exclamations like 'Alas' and 'ah' and phrases like 'suffers', 'heart thump', 'bloodshot', 'dreaming', 'grief-stricken', 'dreams' and 'love' give the poem a strong romantic flavour with parodic intent, evident, for example, in the stereotyped classical connotations of 'hermaphrodite', in the stale mythical allusiveness of 'suffers a change', and in the use of a dead metaphor like 'pillars of salt'. Interestingly, however, the yearning for 'the perfect friends' whose 'ironies make your heart thump' and the desperate cry 'yes he is alive, too' simultaneously show Ackroyd using emotive language in a serious, unembarrassed way, thus evincing what can be described as a paradoxical anxious playfulness that, according to Edward Larrissy, is characteristic of postmodernist 'language' poets. According to Larrissy, the maturation of these poets would depend precisely on their understanding that they should 'cease to disavow Romanticism in the anxious way that has been such a notable feature of our era'.[18]

In other words, the poem as a whole can be read as the avant-garde poet's parody of the humanist lamenting the death of poetry, his mockery of the snobbish feeling of isolation from 'the grief-stricken multitudes' of the romantic poet, and his scorning of the latter's boastful feeling of superiority as he launches into mature life, to 'obtain the world'. Or it can be read as Peter Ackroyd's romanticized and subjective memory of a life experience at a particularly crucial moment, when he left his university friends at Cambridge to go to Yale, at the time of his climactic passage from boyhood to adulthood made more painful by the dark memory of the absent father, and the defiant affirmation of homosexuality ('yes he is alive, too'), that suggests a deeply felt insecurity.

Although the poem is divided into seven stanzas, the length of the lines and the fact that they do not rhyme give it a rhythm comparable to the natural rhythm of prose, recalling Ackroyd's remark in *Notes for a New Culture* that Frank O'Hara's attempts to use language creatively often result in 'the enlargement of line and a loosening of structure that engages a kind of poetic language' (*NNC* 129). Many poems in the early collections show a similar tendency to enlarge the line and to assume the rhythm of prose and even to become poetic prose *tout court*, as happens for example with the third poem in *Ouch*, 'Scenes from Modern Life', a piece of poetic prose that combines an external narrator's report of a boy's reflections away from home with extracts from a letter written by the boy himself to his mother. Likewise, 'Country Life' (*CL*), as we have seen, is a prose sketch containing the dream of a patient called Jeremy, and the analysis of the dream by his psychoanalyst. Another interesting example of prose poem is 'Lovers But Still Strangers', first published in *London Lickpenny*. A female speaker, Lita, muses on her estrangement from her earlier lover, Garth, and her new attachment to Monty, in a style that combines echoes of the romantic style of cheap novelettes ('He did not know that everything I said was for his own sake. I felt tears wet my lashes [...] "Please Lita," he begged, "you're driving me crazy. You know I love you"'), with unexpectedly neat, original and quite witty expressions ('You could have stirred my knees with a spoon'). Lita's pseudo-romantic idiolect strongly recalls that of Gerty in the 'Nausicaa' episode of *Ulysses*, an episode that Ackroyd expressly mentions in *Notes for a New Culture* as an extraordinary example of virtuosity in 'the creation of a self-sustained world of language' (*NNC* 62). In other words, in 'Lovers But Still Strangers' Ackroyd parodies Joyce's parody of the romantic style of cheap novelettes, thus ironically taking the self-begetting free play of language a step further from the point where Joyce had left it.

The same kind of romantic style is parodied in another prose poem entitled 'Foolish Tears' (*LL*). The poem is spoken by the anonymous author of a poem entitled 'Foolish Tears'. As the narrator–author explains, the poem is about a shy young man, very much like himself, called David Watt, who is 'madly in love' with 'a certain girl'. Where in 'Lovers But Still Strangers' we hear the voice of a young woman musing on her love affairs, here we find that the character parodied is the self-admiring author of a poem written as a school exercise consisting of '194 words including title', who thinks very highly of his creative powers ('Even though it was confusing I still enjoyed writing it, and I think I am a good writer').

The fact that many of Ackroyd's poems in the four collections are narrative poems with more or less consistent paraphrasable content has important theoretical implications, for it shows Ackroyd yielding to the temptation to move away from a purely empty 'language poetry' and back to the more traditional 'poetry of things', where, for all the mechanisms to disguise it, the voice of the narrator is perforce heard, offering the reader his subjective vision of the world. From the point of view of Ackroyd's development as a writer, we may say that his tendency to write narrative poems and to draw attention to problems of perception and perspective align him with poets emerging in Britain and Northern Ireland in the late sixties and seventies such as James Fenton, Paul Muldoon and Tom Paulin, who, according to Blake Morrison and Andrew Motion,[19] are likewise characterized by a combined interest in narrative and in the self-conscious foregrounding of the narrative process itself. On the other hand, Ackroyd's recurrent use of parody, pastiche and direct allusion even in the poems with more thematic coherence (also a characteristic trait in the later poetry of Muldoon), as well as his repeated affirmation of the futility of trying to be original clearly betray the influence of T. S. Eliot.

In *Notes for a New Culture* Ackroyd cites Eliot's radical insight into the nature of the subject in 'Tradition and the Individual Talent'. For Ackroyd, the importance of this essay lies in Eliot's 'awareness of the slightness of that selfhood which emerges through the language of poetry' (*NNC* 53). For Eliot the 'mind' of the poet is an invisible 'catalyst' through which individual feelings are combined and transformed into certain 'universal' forms. Eliot, therefore, would use an impersonal and atemporal voice, whose context is the past of written language, the whole literary tradition to which the poet belongs. According to Ackroyd, Eliot employs allusion and quotation at maximum pressure in *The Waste Land*, not as mere rhetorical devices, but as a way of freeing language completely: 'Eliot employs the language of ballads, direct quotations, pastiche, generalized commentary and narrative, and even rag-time, [as a way of giving language] an autonomy, a proper life that exists beyond the customary Anglo-Saxon context of connotation and meaning' (*NNC* 56).

Like Eliot, Ackroyd builds his poems on allusion, parody, pastiche and the ironic rewriting of earlier texts, as a language liberating mechanism, creating what might be described as self-conscious linguistic palimpsests of the accumulated echoes of his favourite modernist predecessors; among others Ezra Pound, W. B. Yeats, W. H. Auden, Dylan Thomas, James Joyce, and, above all, T. S. Eliot. A poem such as 'This beautiful fruit' (*LL*), for example, combines an allusion to Yeats's 'Sailing to Byzantium' in the first stanza ('so now I go sailing into the empyrean/ where my poems may glitter like cars'), with another to Gerard Manley Hopkins ('Just look up at the stars! The stars!'), in the last line of the first stanza, and to W. H. Auden's 'Spain' ('Yes, they are dead'), in the first line of the second stanza.

Echoes of Eliot are also evident in 'on the third...' (*LL*). The first two lines ('on the third stroke/ it will be uncertain') combine Eliot's words from 'The Burial of the Dead' 'on the final stroke of nine',[20] and from 'The Dry Salvages': 'In the uncertain hour before the morning'.[21] The words also bring to mind the telephone speaking clock ('on the third stroke it will be five past nine precisely'), an oblique acknowledgement, perhaps, of Eliot's interest in the mechanization of subjectivity, including time, in contemporary life.

An example of even more elaborate pastiche from *The Waste*

17

Land appears in the second stanza of 'the novel' (*DP*). As is well known, in 'The Burial of the Dead' Eliot subverts tradition by parodying the first lines of the 'Prologue' to *The Canterbury Tales* ('Whan that Aprille with his shoures soote/ The droghte of March hath perced to the roote'), in his memorable beginning: 'April is the cruellest month, breeding/ Lilacs out of the dead land'.[22] In 'the novel' Ackroyd acknowledges indebtedness to the medieval tradition, to Eliot and to Ezra Pound, with a triple allusion:

> So winter is coming in and the self fades
> and flickers, we read novels late into the night
> watching helplessly as characters race toward each other
> until the screams and whistles finally die down
> and a faint violet spreads across the margin.

The first line brings to mind the anonymous lyrical poem 'Sumer is i-cumen in' (*c.* 1240), a well-known medieval paean hailing the coming of spring ('sumer') after the bleak and dark winter, through Ezra Pound's parodic rewriting of it ('Winter is i-cumen in'). The second echoes Marie's bored words at the end of the first stanza of 'The Burial of the Dead': 'I read, much of the night, and go south in the winter'.[23] Likewise, the speaker's activity of reading until 'a faint violet spreads across the margin' brings to mind 'the violet hour, when the eyes and back/ Turn upward from the desk' from 'The Fire Sermon'.[24] Indebtedness to Eliot may be traced also in the narrator's comment in the first stanza that 'outside the girls are singing "Ragtime"', one of Eliot's favourite rhythms. But Eliot and Pound are not the only preceding masters alluded to. As the narrator ponders on how to write a novel, he wishes he 'could immortalise [...] these people [...]/ like Ronald Firbank or even Graham Greene', but feels incapable of going beyond their achievement, or that of Thomas Hardy, as the reference to Angel Clare (from *Tess of the D'Urbervilles*) makes clear:

> So much has been written about this light, both for
> and against. I don't know how to begin –
> where the stars go? how the day starts?
> Angel Clare bows his head against the wind,
> thinking about the things he has to do today.

Interestingly, the 'people' the lyrical subject would like to

18

immortalize are 'wearing sweaters saying "Crisis? What Crisis"'. In other words, they are the followers of the Labour Party prime minister Jim Callaghan, who pronounced those unfortunate words on his return from an international conference to a Britain suffering the 'winter of discontent'. The catchphrase 'Crisis? What Crisis?' is notoriously seen as the key insouciance that led to Thatcher winning in 1979. Therefore, the lyrical subject's complaint that he cannot aspire to 'immortalise [...] these people' is cunningly contradicted in practice by this deft synthetic portrayal of the members of the Labour Party.

Likewise, the acknowledgement that the description of the light as 'violet' is not original, and that he cannot write another story about 'star-crossed' lovers without taking into account the versions of the earlier masters, makes the would-be writer wonder about his own identity. The poem ends with a self-directed question ('if I come out into the open will I be myself,/ or will it be the beginning of another story'). However, the poem emerges from its echoes to stand on its own two feet as a rather original poem by a young writer painfully aware of what Harold Bloom has called the 'anxiety of influence', the tension felt by the contemporary poet between, on the one hand, his realization that everything has already been written because he comes at the tail-end of a very long tradition of writing, and, on the other, his need to add to this tradition his own original contribution, even if knowing all the while that language can only imperfectly communicate meaning, and is the source, not the product, of the writer's subjectivity.

In a first reading, Ackroyd's poetry as a whole would appear to stem from this conviction that the only activity left to the contemporary poet is to recover the words of the past and to rearrange them into empty linguistic patterns, devoid of human content or values. Reduced to the category of linguistic constructions, feelings like tenderness or love can exist only in the mind, as conceptual abstractions, and can only be evoked as concrete arrangements of words or 'patterns'. This is the subject matter of 'Only connect...' (LL), a poem whose title echoes both E. M. Forster's epigraph to Howard's End, 'Only connect...' and T. S. Eliot's allusion to it in 'The Fire Sermon',[25] 'I can connect/ Nothing with nothing':

> Only connect
> sounds of love
>   come from the head
>   in a fixed handwriting
>   name following name

However, in section vi of the same poem, the narrator indulges in the idea that his poetry might after all be original and capable of conveying values and experiences significant to other people: 'The consumers in the great urban centre/ heard this song and were moved by it [...] It was an idea which had not been discovered'. In another late poem, entitled 'the day...' (*DP*), Ackroyd likewise rejects the self-conscious emptiness of 'language poetry'. The lyrical 'I', after attempting to describe a particular experience on a particular day, hopes that he has succeeded in imitating Eliot, but disagrees with the master's lack of emotional involvement: 'I think this is what Eliot meant/ except that I don't think/ the words are short/ in the mouth/ tranquility is not one of them'. These lines bring to mind Henry Reed's parody of *The Waste Land*, 'Chard Whitlow', in *A Map of Verona* (1946), when the speaker tells Eliot: 'I think you will find this put,/ Far better than I could ever hope to express it,/ In the words of Kharma.'[26] Significantly, Ackroyd's allusion lacks the humorous element of Reed's parody. In yet another late poem, 'watching the process...' (*DP*), Ackroyd's growing impatience with his allotted task as builder of meaningless and derivative linguistics patterns finally gives way to the acknowledgement that poetry should be capable of expressing human values and communicating the experience of the socially aware, moral self, defended by aesthetic humanism, that Eliot's

> 'each thing in its own season'
> and such sophistication
>   is fine in green times
>   but in this place
> where no one has a home?

Clearly, the fragment also betrays Ackroyd's 'anxiety of influence', the pressure exerted on his writing by Eliot's poetry in general and by *Four Quartets* in particular.

I suggested at the beginning that Ackroyd's rearrangement of his earlier poems in *The Diversions of Purley* apparently followed an arbitrary order. However, behind its apparent arbitrariness it is now possible to see how carefully he has arranged the poems thematically, in order to suggest an increasing tension between, on the one hand, his theoretical commitment to the modernist ideas defined in *Notes for a New Culture* and to the writing of language poetry and, on the other, his growing need to use language as an instrument for the communication of human experience and values. It is not perhaps by sheer chance, then, that the last but one poem in *The Diversions of Purley* should be a poem from *Country Life*, entitled 'there are so...', a poem in which the lyrical 'I' acutely feels his own self-fragmentation and alienation from the world, in the prison-house of language:

> I suppose this is a definition of madness
> being detached from life and yet needing it
> so that the smallest resentment can kill
> and the poet drifts morosely into the evening
>
> which never satisfies him, while sober,
> but which he may choose to write 'about'.

The Audenesque flavour of these lines acquires existentialist overtones in the next stanza, as the lyrical subject echoes Stragon's opening remark in *Waiting for Godot*, 'Nothing to be done': 'and there is nothing to be done/ except to go on to the next task, and then the next'. The solution the narrator offers the reader in the first stanza ('there are so many emotions to get through/ that I dream continually of slipping backwards/ while the day spins ahead of me like a kite/ although its string leads precisely nowhere'), amounts to the recuperation of 'life' by means of the imaginative recreation of a past that need not even be real, a solution that points to the true source of Ackroyd's imagination and brings to mind Linda Hutcheon's contention in *A Poetics of Postmodernism*,[27] that postmodernist art is fundamentally contradictory and that postmodernist literature is simultaneously self-conscious while yet managing to reconnect the readers to the world outside the page.

It is in this light that 'the diversions of Purley', the poem after which the latest collection is named, acquires full significance. Ackroyd has borrowed this title from John Horne Tooke's three-volume study on language, published in 1786–1805. Tooke (1736–1812) was a popular philologist, much admired by James

21

Mill and the Utilitarians, although his philosophical – rather than historical or philological – approach to language led him to coin wildly speculative etymologies. Ackroyd's title, therefore, might be taken to function as a warning to the reader that he feels as free as John Horne Tooke to create his own wildly speculative and meaningless linguistic patterns. This interpretation is apparently fostered by the beginning of 'the diversions of Purley' (*DP*). In the opening lines, the poet's fight for originality and self identity has become a lost battle that kills the poet's romantic dreams of fulfilment and self-assertion:

> Your writing is peaceful now, and so starve
> Your dream which looked at itself and drowns
> When Mr Harding reached the parsonage he
> Found that the arch-deacon had been called away
> And a natural hush falls over us,

The poet's incapacity to be original is deftly expressed through the combination of allusions which suffuse the story he is writing: 'When Mr Harding reached the parsonage he/ Found that the arch deacon had been called away' bring to mind the rhythm and register of 'If you see dear Mrs Equitone,/ Tell her I bring the horoscope myself', from 'The Burial of the Dead'.[28] What is more, the reference to 'Mr Harding', repeated in the second stanza with a literal quotation ('how can we pretend to describe/ The rapture with which Mr Harding was received?'), adds a new set of allusions: Mr Harding could be the Revd Septimus Harding, a character in Anthony Trollope's Barsetshire novels, although perhaps it is just a pseudo-reference – like the ones used by Eliot in 'Gerontion' – if this Mr Harding is the 'Mr Lewis Harding' that appears in 'the rooks' (*LL*). The possibility that Mr Harding's name might be just a name chosen at random from the Borgesian Library of Babel would be in keeping with the poem's message that the poet's creative activity is only a mechanical task impossibly aimed at the endless re-writing of the all-encompassing textual universe:

> oh repeat that
> Repeat until the billion names of God
> Put out the firmament and the stones cry
> Ma Ba Ta. The sermon is now complete it is a

22

> Vague hush as your mechanical song
> Fills the garden, and the leaves turn red
> And then black.

In an unexpected development, the speaker's mechanical song, repeated *ad infinitum* like Buddhist mantras, and endlessly recombined like the alphabetic symbols in Borges's 'The Library of Babel', suddenly acquires the transcendental power of cabbalistic gematria to rearrange the 'billion names of God'. As Richard Cavendish[29] recalls, according to the Cabbala, the twenty-two Hebrew letters are associated with the twenty-two works of creation in Genesis and are believed to contain all wisdom, all truth, all knowledge of God and the universe. By mastering the hidden wisdom contained in the alphabet man can master the universe and himself become God. Therefore, by endlessly repeating all possible combinations of the alphabet ('The sermon is now complete'), the speaker hopes to put an end to the cosmogonic cycle in which he is trapped ('Put out the firmament'), and to recover the atemporal moment of perfect unity of God and cosmos ('it is a/ Vague hush [...] and the leaves turn red/ And then black'), when stones (the simplest form of matter and, therefore, all forms of creation), participated in it, as suggested by their ability to recite the (Arabic) alphabet ('the stones cry/ Ma Ba Ta').

In 'the diversions of Purley', therefore, we see Ackroyd attempting to get out of the modernist prison-house of language in a characteristically contradictory way that evinces the influence of Pound and Eliot. He affirms the constructedness of writing while simultaneously attempting to recover its mythopoeic and transcendental function. As we will see, this attempt to recuperate the (unreal and fictional) texts of the past as a way of conferring meaning on the present and of achieving self-identity is to become the pivot around which Ackroyd's novels will develop.

2

Lord of Language and Lord of Life

When choosing his curriculum as an undergraduate at Cambridge Ackroyd tried to avoid fiction to such a degree that, as he told an interviewer: 'I don't think I even *read* a novel till I was 26 or 27'.[1] Although, in a later interview, he softened this statement, admitting that he had written a thesis on James Baldwin, Richard Wright and Ralph Ellison,[2] the fact remains that he was not seriously interested in fiction until 1973, when he became the youngest literary editor ever employed by the *Spectator*. Ackroyd then started reading fiction with the same voracity with which he had been reading poetry and literary theory at Cambridge and Yale. In 1978 he began writing *Dressing Up: Transvestism and Drag, the History of an Obsession* (1979) and was gathering material for his first biography, *Ezra Pound and his World* (1980). In keeping with his belief that all kinds of writing are simply the free play of language, Ackroyd sees his evolution from poetry to biography and fiction writing as complementary aspects of the same endeavour: 'I do not see any great disjunction, or any great hiatus between the poetry and the fiction. For me they are part of the same process. Similarly the biographies. I don't think of biographies and fictions as being separate activities.'[3]

As the subtitle makes clear, in *Dressing Up* Ackroyd sets out to investigate the origins, evolution and diverse degrees of acceptance or rejection by different cultures of a recurrent phenomenon whose roots go back to the dawn of mankind and is traceable in widely divergent types of civilization. *Dressing Up* is a well documented, fully illustrated survey of transvestism and drag which already shows the young writer's interest in the comic possibilities cross-dressing offers the performing arts in general and pantomime in particular. This topic will find its more complex expression in *Dan Leno and the Limehouse Golem* (1994), but all his fiction may be said to evince with greater or lesser intensity a clear interest in transvestism and drag, reflected, for example, in the construction of grotesque and ludicrous gay or lesbian secondary characters or of heterosexual characters related to the world of music hall.

At the same time, Ackroyd had been working on *Ezra Pound and his World* (1980) and was soon to begin work on his first two novels, *The Great Fire of London* (1982) and *The Last Testament of Oscar Wilde* (1983), and on his second biography, *T. S. Eliot* (1984). In chapter 1 we saw how Ackroyd's poetry evinces a growing impatience with the astringencies of poststructuralist and deconstructive theory and how he attempted to go beyond the modernist 'inward turn' in late poems such as 'the diversions of Purley' by having recourse to the mythopoeic and transcendental function of writing. Therefore, his biographies of Ezra Pound and T. S. Eliot, written earlier than these poems, may be said to respond to Ackroyd's need to analyse the ways in which the two great modernist poets had approached and tried to solve the same question, while *The Great Fire of London* and *The Last Testament of Oscar Wilde* may be described as Ackroyd's first reactions to Pound's and Eliot's imaginative solutions.

Like *Dressing Up*, the biography of Ezra Pound was conceived as an introductory book, aimed at the general reader. Although the text is, therefore, limited in extension and allows the author little space for elaborate argumentation, it shows Ackroyd's fascination for the way in which the great modernist 'often elicits great poetry from the manipulation of another's voice' (*DU* 53), and how he managed to express his 'restless and shifting identity' translating, reshaping and manipulating the voices of the past masters into what can be described as an intertextual palimpsest of accumulated echoes, capable of suggesting a self-sustained world of language, precisely, as we saw in chapter 1, the effect that Ackroyd had been trying to achieve in his own poetry.

In *A Draft of XXX Cantos*, Ezra Pound presents the poet as wandering Odysseus, a mythical quester travelling across time zones and ontological boundaries in order to 'shock the readers [...] into an awareness of the disturbed and complex world around them' (*EPW* 75). Pound's method to suggest the existence of a 'disturbed and complex' outward ontology is carried out through juxtapositions: of the general with the particular, of all kinds of 'voices', genres and modes, and of history, autobiography and literature. Although the *Cantos* were left unfinished and are made up of fragmented extracts demanding the reader's collaboration to complete them, Pound was convinced that they contained 'all the knowledge worth knowing, all the works of literature worth reading',[4] thus gesturing to a mysterious unity-within-fragmentation, which brings to mind T. S. Eliot's – and Peter Ackroyd's – need to find the underlying pattern holding together the fragmentary and subjective perceptions of the thinking individual.

In the biography of T. S. Eliot, Ackroyd explains how Pound and Eliot shared an acute feeling of alienation from American culture and society that produced in them 'a terrible emptiness' and the need to seek for 'a tradition or order of their own' (*TSE* 25). Eliot's need to find 'some centre, some kind of coherence or wholeness' (*TSE* 25) is surely what lies at the heart of Pound's baffling unity-within-fragmentation effect in the *Cantos*. And, according to Ackroyd, it is also what explains Eliot's early fascination with the philosophical ideas of F. H. Bradley, on which he wrote his doctoral thesis.

Convinced of the relativity and subjectivity of meaning and of the impossibility of discovering any objective meaning even in the most significant patterns of human behaviour, Eliot seeks a way out of pure subjectivity and the failure of communication it involves, by embracing Bradley's definition of reality: 'For Bradley "Reality is One", a seamless and coherent whole which is non-relational – that is, it cannot be divided into separate intellectual categories' (*TSE* 49). As Ackroyd further explains, in his subversion of such orthodox categories as 'space' and 'time', which reflect only a partial comprehension of reality, 'Bradley is pushed back towards a larger description which can only be expressed as the Absolute. Without such a concept, the world becomes literally meaningless. The Absolute holds together Thought and Reality, Will and Feeling, in a sublime whole' (*TSE* 49).

Bradley's contention that 'Reality is One' and that there is an Absolute truth in the realm of the sublime, beyond the limitations of conceptual knowledge, brings to mind Emerson's pantheistic idealism. However, in Bradley's scheme idealism is combined with the kind of scepticism that was so dear to Eliot, the recognition that all forms of knowledge and experience are conditional or relative, and that it is only when 'they are organized into a coherent whole [that] they can vouchsafe glimpses of absolute truth' (TSE 50). Ackroyd points out, in words that recall his own 'magpie acquisitiveness' and go a long way towards explaining the structural neatness of his novels, that 'the only way of reaching towards the Absolute is by a steady enlargement of our knowledge and a continual search for system, unity and coherence' (TSE 50).

In the ensuing novels, we will see how Ackroyd attempts to transcend the modernist 'inward turn' along the lines set by Pound and Eliot, that is, by postulating the transcendental component of writing, but we will also see how extremely difficult he finds it to pledge his trust in the existence of an absolute and transcendental ideal world, for, as he notes in the Eliot biography, the problem with this scheme is that it is based on an act of faith, the postulation of the existence of an Absolute Logos, an objective world in which, in F. H. Bradley's words, 'the cruder and vaguer, or more limited, is somehow contained and explained in the wider and precise' (TSE 70).

Ackroyd's first published novel, The Great Fire of London (1982), was received by the critics as an interesting development in the career of the poet and already well-known 'incisive and abrasive reviewer'.[5] The Great Fire of London is the first of a whole series of fictional and non-fictional books prompted by Ackroyd's admiration for Dickens, to whom he devotes his formidable, 1,195-page-long biography Dickens (1990).

Structurally, the novel follows the characteristic multiplot pattern of Victorian fiction. In the first four chapters of Part One, an external narrator introduces in succession each of the different main characters: Little Arthur, Audrey Skelton, Spenser Spender and Rowan Phillips. The ensuing chapters progressively develop the complex net of relationships that knit together the lives of these four main characters to each other and to innumerable other characters whose paths meet either because

27

they are interested in making a film version of *Little Dorrit*, like Spenser and Phillips, or because they live in the area where the plot of *Little Dorrit* was set, like Little Arthur and Audrey Skelton.

As the plot develops, the more intuitive characters come to realize that they are only the latest generation living in an area of London that has been inhabited for thousands of years in an unbroken chain of successive generations of men and women whose traces are still recognizable on the faces of the people as well as in the alleys, the squares and the buildings frequented by them. Some vaguely intuit that they are somehow connected to the past of the city and that a better understanding of the history of London would help them come to terms with themselves.

This feeling of 'transhistorical connectedness' is expressed in the names of the characters. Spenser Spender's name, for example, simultaneously evokes the poet of the thirties Stephen Spender, the founder of evolutionist philosophy Herbert Spencer, and the Renaissance poet Edmund Spenser. Likewise, Little Arthur's name simultaneously evokes Little Dorrit and Arthur Clennam, while Audrey's friend Pally, a half-wit with a drooping mouth, would be the contemporary equivalent of Amy Dorrit's friend Maggie. Another of the main characters, the script writer Rowan Phillips, is a Cambridge-based Canadian academic and novelist with a passion for Dickens who may be described as a parodic version of Peter Ackroyd (*GFL* 19). But the most complex example of transhistorical or 'reincarnated' character is Audrey Skelton, the telephone operator whom Rowan Phillips believes to be schizophrenic because she is constantly day-dreaming and has memories from the past, like the one in which she 'remembers' the fire that destroyed the Marshalsea Prison on 14 December 1885 (*GFL* 25), that is, about the time when Dickens started writing *Little Dorrit*. Audrey had a crucial experience the day she attended a seance near Ealing Common and was invaded by the spirit of Little Dorrit. From then on, Amy Dorrit starts speaking through her and Audrey believes herself to be the Victorian heroine.

Another character obsessed with Dickens is Spenser Spender, whose project of filming *Little Dorrit* is based on his belief that 'Dickens understood London', and he is convinced that the film might help him solve some kind of mystery connecting London to his own life. Indeed, the film maker is fascinated with the ancient city, and the weird power it exerts over him:

'There's something strange about London, love... [...] I'm sure there's something to it, some kind of magic or something. Did you know if you drew a line between all of Hawksmoor's churches, they would form a pentangle?' (GFL 16)

The idea the drunken film maker is trying to transmit to his bored wife, Laetitia, is that London has a transhistorical mystical and/or magical side whose spirit Dickens succeeded in capturing in his fiction. His theory perfectly complements the impression produced by the characters' names that they are transhistorical types, made up of accumulated literary and historical echoes.

The characters who are involved in the film project, like Rowan Phillips, Job Penstone (the Victorian academic), and Sir Frederick Lustlambert (the director of the Film Financial Board), are interested in Dickens as a means of recovering London's history. However, as Spender is surprised to discover, their approaches to Little Dorrit are puzzlingly divergent and incompatible with his own interpretation: 'each time a new interpretation of Little Dorrit was sprung upon him, it subtly devalued his own and it took a conscious effort of will for him to reassert it' (GFL 85). Interestingly, a similar feeling invades Little Arthur, Pally and Audrey Skelton, that is, the characters who appear to be the reincarnations of the Victorian protagonists, as well as the numberless outcasts that crowd the Marshalsea prison and the nearby area of London where the exteriors of Little Dorrit are being filmed. Eventually, these characters (and also the tramps) become convinced that they must put an end to the filming of Little Dorrit because the film is hopelessly 'misreading' the real spirit of London. As soon as Audrey makes up her mind to burn down the stage by the river where the exteriors are being filmed, the tramps enthusiastically agree to help her set fire to it (GFL 162).

Within a realistic logic, the reader instinctively assumes an ontological difference between the 'real' world in which Ackroyd's characters move and the 'fictional' world of Dickens's characters. Therefore, the transmigration of the soul of Little Dorrit to the body of Audrey Skelton can only take place if we

29

accept either the 'fictionality' of the visionary telephone operator, or the 'reality' of the Dickensian character. The same ontological incongruence lies behind the assumption that Audrey Skelton might be a 'reincarnation' of a real Renaissance poet, or Spenser Spender of various real writers and thinkers. Therefore, the only possibility would be to accept the fact that, in the world of *The Great Fire of London*, the boundaries between fiction and reality are nonexistent, that the difference between 'fictional' characters and 'real' people, and between 'real' and 'fictional' worlds, simply does not hold.

This interpretation gives the novel a baffling *regressus in infinitum* structure that enhances its condition of *writing*: Peter Ackroyd writes a sequel to *Little Dorrit* in which Rowan Phillips writes a script of *Little Dorrit*, for Spenser Spender's film version of *Little Dorrit*, to which Job Penstone and Sir Frederick Lustbambert would like to contribute their own versions of *Little Dorrit*, all of which are equally subjective and distorted 'misreadings' of the original novel. Thus, *The Great Fire of London* reveals its condition of an autonomous and self-begetting linguistic universe, endlessly yielding different versions of itself and constantly begetting derivative characters and derivative authors alike.

As the novel reveals its textuality, the liberation of the reincarnated Dickensian characters by the 'great fire' with which the novel ends loses its apocalyptic dimension and becomes the futile rebellion of unfree fictional characters against their god-like creator: they succeed in burning their way out of the cardboard prison-house of Spenser Spender's film version of their world only, however, to find themselves trapped within the walls of Peter Ackroyd's textual world. But the joke is two-edged, for also imprisoned within the cardboard walls of the novel and incapable of conceiving his own transcendental escape is the god-like Author himself, whose fictionality is suggested by the identification of Ackroyd with Phillips and the fact that his own version of *Little Dorrit* is an equally distorted and subjective 'misreading' of Dickens's original text.

To sum up, in *The Great Fire of London* Ackroyd writes his own overtly literary and fragmentary version of *Little Dorrit* and attempts to unify it, presenting London as a transhistorical mythical city gathering together the wisdom of the English race at large. Incapable, however, of making the crucial act of faith in a transcendental Absolute Logos, Ackroyd, in a characteristic metafictional twist, eventually destroys the painfully built illusion of transcendence, revealing the textual nature of the mythical London just created, thus condemning himself with his characters to the isolation and seclusion of the 'prison-house of language'. Time and again, Ackroyd will try to find a way out in every new novel, progressively refining his own imaginative answer to the modernist 'inward turn'.

In keeping with the modernist definition of writing as 'free play', Ackroyd, in *The Last Testament of Oscar Wilde* (1983), consciously blurs the boundaries between biography and fiction: he assumes the voice and style of his much admired Irish writer and aesthete in order to write a 'fictional autobiography'. In it Oscar Wilde is supposed to give his 'own' version of the events that led to the scandal and trial that ended with Wilde's imprisonment and ruin, with his social ostracism, the estrangement from his family and his premature death in exile. In a characteristic pendular swing, Ackroyd will likewise 'fictionalize' his most ambitious biography, *Dickens* (1990), undercutting the traditional chronological arrangement of the narration of Dickens's life from birth to death by the interpolation of seven metafictional 'Interludes' in which the boundaries between past and present and between the historical events lived by Dickens and the fictional episodes the Victorian writer imagined in his novels are consistently mixed up.

Formally, *The Last Testament of Oscar Wilde* follows the literary tradition of the 'confession' of a repenting sinner. Although, in keeping with this tradition, Wilde's 'confession' is explicitly addressed to a 'you', the reason he gives for writing it is a desire to spell out the truth and real meaning of his life to himself, for, as he reflects, 'I have lied to myself. Now I must try to break the habit of a lifetime' (*LTOW* 3). Structured as a daily journal, Wilde's confession runs from 11 August 1900 to 24 November 1900, includes a few newspaper cuttings from Wilde's lecture tour to the United States (*LTOW* 95–6), and also a series of tales narrated by Wilde that may be said to function as iconic variations on certain episodes in Wilde's life. It ends with the reproduction of his deathbed feverish 'talking taken down by Maurice Gilbert'(*LTOW* 184–5), from 26 November 1900 until the

31

day of his death, 30 November 1900.

Mary Montaut has pointed out how 'The novel is painstakingly researched'.[6] Indeed, a diligent comparison with the standard biographies and collected letters of Oscar Wilde would reveal a surprising exactness and the sheer bulk of the biographical data contained in the novel. This, together with the wonderfully accurate effect produced by the clever stylistic imitation of Wilde's witty, paradoxical and ironic style, function as strong realism-enhancing mechanisms that forcefully impel the reader to sympathize with Oscar Wilde – that is, to 'pardon his sins' – and to lament the fact that the novel does not have a happy ending as 'Ackroyd plainly wants Wilde to have'.[7]

At the same time, however, Wilde's narration is rendered in wholly literary terms, as a Faustian descent into hell originally motivated by the aesthetic desire to 'sin beautifully', to try all forms of sensual pleasure as a way of refining his intelligence. Wilde narrates his transformation from aristocrat and artist to convict and tramp as a pilgrimage along the labyrinthine and dark recesses of a London that is presented as mythical and atemporal (*LTOW* 108). And, describing his fateful relationship with Bosie (Lord Alfred Taylor), he underlines the decisive role played by his imagination in their sensual pursuit of pleasure and the progressive unreality of the whole relationship and of the city itself, in words that bring to mind *The Waste Land* and *The Picture of Dorian Gray*:

> As we became more frenzied in our pursuit of pleasure, London itself became an unreal city, a play of brilliant lights and crowds and mad laughter. My boldness infected Bosie [...]. He wished to become precisely the portrait of him which I had formed in my imagination and so he became terrible, because my imagination was terrible also. (*LTOW* 127)

Musing about his impending death, Wilde wonders whether he will remain alive in the memory of the people, or whether his martyrdom, like that of St Procopius, will be 'wonderfully increased by each succeeding legend'. He concludes that distortion of the historical facts is inevitable, that, as soon as Maurice starts to take down what he is dictating, 'he will invent my last hours'. That is, Wilde is perfectly aware that each successive version of his life will be the subjective 'misreading' of each future biographer. However, unlike Spenser Spender or Audrey Skelton, he is not at all worried by this prospect and, in fact, prefers the 'misreadings' to the original version, as he believes that 'it was the legends that worked the miracles, not the bones.' (*LTOW* 180).

A few days before his death, Wilde remembers the picture of a prince he has seen in the Louvre and wishes he could go back to that past, that he could 'enter another man's heart', for, as he explains, 'In that moment of transition, when I was myself and someone else, of my own time and in another's, the secrets of the universe would stand revealed' (*LTOW* 181). His ironic suggestion that he wishes he could assume the personality of the figure in a picture, and not the other way round – as happened in *The Picture of Dorian Gray* – may be read as evidence that he believes Art to be a life-giving and superior form of reality, and it is clear that he considers this kind of transcendence a form of illumination, for as he approaches the hour of his death, he 'long[s] to enter the noisy thoroughfares and dilapidated courtyards of Balzac's imagination' (*LTOW* 181), and he dies laughing with joy in the knowledge that 'then once more I shall be lord of language and lord of life' (*LTOW* 185).

In other words, while Bradley and Eliot felt the need to postulate an Absolute Logos in the realm of the Sublime, capable of transcending the limitations of conceptual knowledge and of granting an overall vision of reality as 'One', for Wilde, the aesthete, the Absolute Logos simply becomes Absolute Beauty, and the realm of the sublime, the World of Art, an equally unitary, atemporal and ideal world, which, however, does not exist on a higher, metaphysical plane, but rather on the human plane of the imagination.

This is the lesson Oscar Wilde teaches Ackroyd. From Wilde's aesthetic viewpoint, the artistic (or textual) world created by Peter Ackroyd, entitled *The Last Testament of Oscar Wilde* would become the very higher plane of being towards which Wilde has managed to make his transcendental escape. Thus, by imagining Wilde's migration to an abstract and absolute World of Art made up of the sum total of the voices, styles and visions of the artists and thinkers in the Western canon, Ackroyd manages to suggest the possibility of transcendence without having to postulate the existence of a metaphysical plane of being above or beyond the artistic (or textual) realm itself. In this sense, Peter Ackroyd's accurate and loving recreation of the style and voice of Oscar Wilde in *The Last Testament of Oscar Wilde* provides conclusive evidence that Ackroyd's 'strong predecessor' did manage to transcend his mortality, entering the heart and the mind of the younger writer, and continues speaking through him, as Little Dorrit did through Audrey Skelton.

Ackroyd will give a further turn of the screw to this interesting possibility in *Chatterton* (1987), Ackroyd's most metafictional historiographic metafiction, and a novel that shares with the poetry collections the same deep concerns with the linguistic nature of writing, the Derridean slippage of meaning and the troubled relationship of the individual writer with the literary tradition s/he is inscribed in.

At the beginning of the novel, we see the protagonist, Charles Wychwood following the promptings of an odd 'small sign beside a blue door that reads: "Leno Antiques". Don't Linger. Make Us Very Happy. Walk Up. Do' (C. 8). Entering 'Leno Antiques', Charles finds himself transported from the world of everyday to the fantastic world of a parodic Dickensian 'Old Curiosity Shop'. The owners, Mr and Mrs Leno, are a grotesque couple whose behaviour demonstrates clear Dickensian and 'Punch and Judy' traits, with the name 'Leno' signalling them as direct descendants of Dan Leno, 'the great pantomime dame, comic and music-hall star, known as "the funniest man on earth", [who] died in London on the last day of October 1904'.[8] For Ackroyd, Dan Leno – to whom he devotes his eighth novel – is the most charismatic representative of the centuries-old London tradition of the 'monopolylinguist', that is, 'comedians or actors who play a number of quick-change parts in the course of one performance'. As Ackroyd further notes, the word 'monopolylinguist' is meant to express 'a particular London sensibility [...] a living inheritance that has everything to do with the spirit of place and with the nature of the city'. Another great Victorian music-hall comedian was Leno's predecessor, Charles Mathews, who, according to Ackroyd, so impressed Charles Dickens that he recreated Mathews' impersonation of 'Miss Mildew, a lady dressed entirely in white [...] as Miss Havisham, many years later'.

With Ackroyd's words in mind it is easy to see a parallel

between Mathews's and Leno's influence on Dickens and Dickens's influence on Ackroyd's construction of his characters: the Lenos – like Spenser Spender and the other characters in *The Great Fire of London* – are two living palimpsests of accumulated echoes, embodying the essence of what Ackroyd believes to be a specific London sensibility.

But the Lenos are only two of the many grotesque characters that populate the novel. The music-hall tradition of transvestism and drag is literally embodied in the squalid and affectedly feminine old gay wearing 'a leopard-skin leotard with the top of a red track-suit hanging over it' (*C.* 50), called Pat. The most accomplished example of Dickensian-cum-music-hall character is Harriet Scrope, a formerly bestselling novelist who is currently attempting to write her autobiography as a way to come to terms with her writer's block. She has the striking inborn capacity of the London 'monopolylinguist' to assume different roles and voices and to mimic other characters, just for the fun of it. She is indeed Peter Ackroyd's version of Dickens's Miss Havisham, through a cross-breed of Dan Leno's 'Mother Goose' and Punch's Judy: she calls the librarian Philip Slack 'Pip' (*C.* 148); constantly refers to herself as 'Mother' when she talks to her cat; she sticks her tongue out at Charles's son, Edward – like Mr Leno – when the grown-ups' backs are turned (*C.* 182); and, surprised by the unexpected appearance of Charles, she shrieks: 'I thought [. . .] that you were Mr Punch come to get me' (*C.* 38).

Realism-biased reviewers of *Chatterton* resent the overt fictionality not only of grotesque characters like these, but also of more psychologically developed characters like Philip Slack,[9] failing to realize that Ackroyd's construction of characters is not aimed at creating realistic fictional versions of 'real' people, but rather overtly fictional characters like Harriet Scrope, who is perfectly aware of her own fictionality and cherishes it, which does not mean that she considers herself 'unreal': 'You think I'm grotesque, don't you? But I'm not. I'm all too real. I might even bite' (*C.* 227). The further implication, of course, is that, if Harriet Scrope is 'real', so is the textual world she lives in. Indeed, in the world of *Chatterton* the unreality of fiction and the reality of the material world are constantly denied: Harriet's cat snatches and eats the fake bird on her hat, believing it to be real (*C.* 118), and Harriet's definition of reality is 'the invention of unimaginative people' (C. 39). In other words, Harriet Scrope and the other overtly fictional characters exist as such in order to demonstrate the validity of Chatterton's – and Blake's – contention, expressed in the novel by Meredith, that: 'There is nothing more real than words. They are reality' (C. 157).

At the end of *The Last Testament of Oscar Wilde*, the dying Oscar Wilde recalls the portrait of a prince he had seen at the Louvre and he wishes he could 'return to that past – to enter another man's heart' (*LTOW* 181). Likewise, in *Chatterton*, Charles Wychwood, confronted with the 'Portrait of an Unknown Man' that he believes to be Chatterton in middle-life, still living and writing poetry in the various styles of his contemporaries many years after his official death, becomes emotionally involved with the eighteenth-century poet remembered by posterity as the greatest plagiarist in history, and obsessively tries to establish the truth of his discovery, with the result that his received assumptions about authorial originality are totally disrupted for, as he reflects, if his theory were true, then 'half of the poetry of the eighteenth century is probably written by him' (C. 94).

Charles is an unpublished poet who is suffering from writer's block and also from the effects of a brain tumour that gives him terrible headaches as well as hallucinations in which he sees himself split in two (C. 46). However, he has no doubts about the importance of his only slim unpublished poetry collection and, although he believes (with the young Ackroyd) that 'Poetry is the finer art' (C. 149), he – like Wilde – literally feeds on fiction: during the trip to Bristol he keeps eating little rolls of paper torn from his copy of *Great Expectations* (C. 48–9).

Charles's best friend, Philip Slack, works in a public library frequented by people as desperately lonely and shy as himself. This library is a mythical centre of power on which the alienated and mad invariably converge. Surrounded by books in this Ackroydian version of Borges's 'Library of Babel', Philip Slack may be described as a writer suffering from a bad case of Bloomian 'anxiety of influence'. Although he had once attempted to write a novel, he had abandoned it after realizing that 'It had become a patchwork of other voices and other styles, and it was the overwhelming difficulty of recognizing his own voice among them that had led him to abandon the project' (C. 70).

Philip Slack may be said to stand in the position of Ackroyd's 'humanist' poet struggling to make his individual voice heard against the voices of his 'strong predecessors'. His realization that he cannot recognize 'his own voice' in his writing evinces his romantic bias for authorial autonomy and originality. This is why the pressure exerted on him by the texts of the earlier writers materializes in a paralysing writer's block. And this is also why he is panic-stricken by the vision of the all-encompassing linguistic universe where he works: 'if you crossed the threshold into that world, you would be sur-rounded by words; you would crush them beneath your feet, you would knock against them with your head and arms, but if you tried to grasp them they would melt away. Philip did not dare to turn his back upon these books. Not yet' (C. 71).

At the end of the novel, the discovery of the (fake) Chatterton portrait and also of the Bristol papers supposedly written by the mature Chatterton (but in fact written by his publisher, Joynson, out of revengeful spite), will signify the end of Charles Wychwood's and Philip Slack's bias for authorial originality and closure and their liberation from the 'anxiety of influence'. Reading the (ironically false) newly found papers in which Chatterton defended creative plagiarism and confessed that he was the real author of works attributed to 'Mr Gray, Mr Akenside, Mr Churchill, Mr Collins and sundry others' (C. 92), Charles experiences an illumination, the cathartic realization that: 'our whole understanding of eighteenth-century poetry will have to be revised' (C. 127). Once his belief in authorial originality is shattered, he realizes that even the different biographies of Chatterton contained striking discrepancies: 'each biography described a quite different poet: even the simplest observation by one was contradicted by another, so that nothing seemed certain' (C. 127). Charles had initially 'been annoyed by these discrepancies but then he was exhilarated by them: for it meant that anything became possible. If there were no truths, everything was true' (C. 127). This realization amounts to a fulcrum that frees his imagination and makes him feel capable of writing his own, apparently equally spurious, version of Chatterton's memoirs.

Carried by the force of Charles's reasoning, Philip Slack will undergo a similar cathartic liberation from his romantic attachment to the myth of origins. After Charles's death, he realizes that 'there is no real origin for anything. Everything just exists. Everything just exists in order to exist' (*C.* 232). This realization signifies the end of his writer's paralysis: ' "So I tried writing my own novel but it didn't work, you know. I kept on imitating other people. I had no real story, either, but now –" he hesitated – "but now, with this – with Charles' theory – I might be able to –" ' (*C.* 232). Slack's words give an unexpected metafictional twist to the novel, as it opens up the possibility that Slack might have picked up Charles's story as the subject of his novel and so that he might in fact be the fictional author of *Chatterton.*

When Charles found the early nineteenth-century portrait of Chatterton in 'Leno Antiques', he was fascinated by the eyes of the Unknown Man in the picture. After his death, the portrait is taken to Cumberland and Maitland's art gallery. When Stewart Merk, the expert Seymour faker, is asked to 'improve' it, he realizes that the painting 'contained the residue of several different images, painted at various times' (*C.* 205), and, prompted by the ('aesthetic humanist') need to reveal the 'original' figure, tries to remove the successive layers of paint, with the result that the whole portrait melts – the very effect Philip feared would happen to the words, if he tried to seize them (*C.* 71) – but not before revealing a whole gallery of faces (*C.* 228). Thus, the 'fake' Chatterton portrait reveals Chatterton's true face, one made up of the combined faces of the 'strong' poets of the past whose identity he has contributed to create in the same way they have contributed to create him, thus revealing its condition of transhistorical palimpsest. This is the secret Charles had read in the eyes of the Unknown Man and also the vision he had on his first visit to the Tate Gallery, when, looking at the Wallis portrait of Meredith posing as Chatterton, he sees himself assuming Chatterton's recumbent posture, while Mrs Angell (Chatterton's landlady) becomes his wife Vivien's 'shadow' overlooking the scene from the foot of the bed (*C.* 132). A similar vision is granted to Vivien herself, who, unexpectedly coming across the portrait of the Unknown Man in the art gallery where she works, falls in a faint upon the floor (*C.* 205), surely with the shock of recognizing her dead husband's face in that of the Unknown Man. Likewise, when, after Charles's death, his son Edward goes to the Tate Gallery a second time to contemplate Wallis's portrait, he is astonished to find 'his father lying there' (C. 229).

Charles's detectivesque attempt to unearth the 'true' life of Chatterton soon led him to adopt Chatterton's actions, words and ideas, and the same happened to Meredith after posing as a model for Chatterton's portrait. Consequently, both Meredith and Wychwood start to have visions of Chatterton and eventually meet him at the atemporal moment of his/their death/s, in a scene that strikingly recalls both the Horatian topos of transcending mortality through writing and Borges's notion of supra-individual subjectivity/authorship:

> I will not wholly die, then. Two others have joined him – the young man who passes him on the stairs [Meredith] and the young man who sits with bowed head by the fountain [Wychwood] – and they stand silently beside him. I will live for ever, he tells them. They link hands, and bow towards the sun. (C. 234)

At the beginning of the novel, Chatterton appeared to Charles and asked him to cross the threshold from the material world to the atemporal world of literature. As we have seen, this world is an overtly linguistic universe that recalls both Roland Barthes's notion of *pure écriture* and Jorge Luis Borges's self-contained and all-encompassing Library of Babel. Philip was afraid of entering this world because, within it, he could not preserve his autonomy and identity as a writer. However, for Borges the concept of original authorship as defended by the romantics and symbolists would be not only an impossibility, but also an absurdity, for as Worton and Still[10] have pointed out, Borges shares with Montaigne the belief in a kind of eternal supra-individual Spiritual Voice, a composite of the individual voices of all the dead poets, coexisting for ever in an eternal 'now'.

What Montaigne and Borges call the realm of the supra-individual Spiritual Voice, William Blake would call 'The Imagination which Liveth for Ever', which for Blake is the same as the *anthropos*, Man's mystic or cosmic body: 'The Eternal Body of Man is The IMAGINATION'.[11] It is this compound cosmic body-and-voice, made up of the great poets and artists of the past that Chatterton, Meredith and Wychwood joyfully join with linked hands at the end of the novel, thus achieving immortality, not, however, on the higher, metaphysical sphere of Plato's Logos, but simply in the all too human realm of the Creative Imagination, the very realm that still resounds with Nicholas Dyer's (*H.*) and Oscar Wilde's laughter, and also with William Blake's singing,[12] and whose sight made Chatterton smile (*C.* 234). But it must not be forgotten that, although only 'a dream of wholeness, and of beauty', 'the vision is real', and that 'All the yearning and all the unhappiness and all the sickness can be taken away by that vision' (*C.* 152). The words are Charles's, but they are also, undeniably, Peter Ackroyd's.

To sum up, where in *The Great Fire of London*, Ackroyd, incapable of pledging his faith in the existence of an Absolute Logos, had condemned himself with his characters to the isolation and seclusion of the prison-house of language, in *Chatterton* the writer manages to liberate Charles Wychwood from the shackles of time and the 'fall' into history by assuming, with Blake, the transcendental dimension of the human imagination. From now on, Ackroyd will take this idea for granted in every new novel, and will develop it to its ultimate consequences in one of his most Dickensian novels, *English Music* (1992).

In novels like *David Copperfield* or *Great Expectations* an author – narrator–character tells the story of his orphaned life retrospectively, from his childhood to his old age at the present moment of the narration. In *English Music*, the odd-numbered chapters are likewise narrated by the adult Tim Harcombe, who tells the story of his past life over a span of seventy years, from his motherless childhood and youth in the 1920s and 1930s to his (and the novel's) present in 1992. By contrast, in the even-numbered chapters, an apparently anonymous third-person narrator, who might be Tim watching himself as it were from the outside, tells the trance-like dreams or visions that Tim – like Dickens or Blake – was subject to all his life.

During these trances, Tim finds himself caught up in the books or pictures he has just read or contemplated in what may be described as an all encompassing textual world, made up of the sum total of the English literary and artistic canon. Invariably, Tim, like Dickens and Blake, experiences much more vividly the adventures he has in this imaginative world than in the 'real' world outside, and the imaginative life he leads during these trances is much more interesting than his life in time, which is monotonous, drab and – like those of Pip in Dickens's novel – constantly frustrates his 'great expectations'.

During the sessions of 'faith-healing' organized by his father, a famous mesmerist called Clement Harcombe, Tim is invariably used as a medium. However, although his mediumistic powers are extraordinary, Tim is not aware of them and always attributes the faith-healings exclusively to his father. Ironically, Clement Harcombe becomes more and more dependent on him, until he completely loses faith in his own healing capacity. As a result of this loss of faith, he really loses his powers and is unable to recover them until the end of the novel, when, panic-stricken by the possibility that Tim might die, Clement 'placed the palms of his hands against the sides of [Tim's] head' (*EM* 366) and absorbed his son's fever. Clement's newly recovered faith in himself comes to a climax when he tries to heal Tim's friend, Edward Campion, who suffers from terrible spasmodic shakes. He succeeds in healing him but at the cost of his own life, not without realizing, however, that, in Tim's words, 'the power belonged to neither of us separately, but resided in the very fact of inheritance itself' (*EM* 378).

This sentence synthesizes the core of Clement Harcombe's teaching and is the idea around which Peter Ackroyd's novels invariably develop, the conviction that the power to transcend the limitations of this 'fallen world' does not lie in the individual, but is rather a question of 'transhistorical connectedness'.

After the death of Clement Harcombe, Tim, contemplating the smiling face of his dead father, unexpectedly 'saw it changing wondrous wise, and taking on the lineaments of other faces which he knew'. The palimpsest of faces Tim sees (like the faces beneath that of the Unknown Man in Charles Wychwood's picture in *Chatterton*, or also of 'Old Barren One', in *First Light*), revealed the Harcombe lineage 'stretch[ing] back to the beginning' (*EM* 392). It is at this stage that Tim truly understands the meaning of his father's teachings, and this understanding miraculously transforms him from a clownish trickster with 'white make up [...] and a large false flower in my buttonhole' (like the Mints in *First Light*) into a 'thought-reader' and a 'ventriloquist' (*EM* 396). That is, he becomes what Ackroyd would call a genuine 'Cockney' music-hall 'monopolylinguist' who 'soon discovered that I had an ability to "throw" my voice in any direction I pleased [...]. Sometimes there were many voices, and the ring amazed the audience, who were as bewildered as if they had heard various spirits haunting the circus' (*EM* 396).

At the end of the novel, therefore, Tim has developed the very capacity Ackroyd has always been trying to achieve by absorbing and recasting the voices of his 'strong predecessors' in his poetry, biographies and fiction: the capacity to reproduce the very sound of 'English music', the imaginative human equivalent of the music of the spheres, the product of the sum total of the voices of every writer and artist in the history of English civilization. And it is clear that the effect is numinous, for, in Edward Campion's words:

> Only through an act of the imagination can we see the archetypal form dwelling in substance [...]. Past acts or past traditions are not necessarily lost in time, therefore, because they can be recreated in the imagination: *not relived as part of the endless cycle of the generations but restored in their absolute and unchanging essence.* (*EM* 225, my emphasis)

Thus, the novel reveals itself both as a Borgesian Library of Babel and as Blake's Spiritual or Cosmic Body, a paradoxical textual/imaginary world, trapping Ackroyd/the other individual writers in the English canon within its cardboard walls and simultaneously allowing him/them to live/write in unison in the eternal and sublime yet all too human (and specifically English) World of Art created by the power of Peter Ackroyd's imagination.

3

A Dream of Wholeness, and of Beauty

We have seen how, in the novels so far discussed, Ackroyd invariably describes London as a visionary city, whose roots go back to the dawn of civilization. This vision of mythical London or of the mythical origins of the English race is further developed in his most magical and esoteric novels, *Hawksmoor* (1985), *First Light* (1989), *The House of Doctor Dee* (1993) and *Dan Leno and the Limehouse Golem* (1994).

In the Acknowledgements to *Hawksmoor*, Ackroyd gives an important clue for the understanding of the novel when he expresses his 'obligation to Iain Sinclair's poem, *Lud Heat*, which first directed my attention to the stranger characteristics of the London churches'. In the first section of Book One of *Lud Heat*,[1] Sinclair explains how the historical architect Nicholas Hawksmoor, who had been commissioned to rebuild the churches in London and Westminster destroyed by the Great Fire of 1666, planned the churches according to a strict 'geometry of oppositions',[2] capable of producing a 'system of energies, or unit of connection, within the city',[3] similar to those formed by 'the old hospitals, the Inns of Court, the markets, the prisons, the religious houses and the others'.[4] Hawksmoor arranged Christ Church, St George's in-the-East and St Anne's, Limehouse, to form a power-concentrating triangle, while 'St George's, Blooms-bury, and St Alfege's, Greenwich, make up the major pentacle star',[5] – the 'pentangle' Spenser Spender alludes to in *The Great Fire of London* (p. 16).

Sinclair's vision of London as an intricate net of emblematic buildings accumulating through time the occult power of its millenarian inhabitants is the basic idea around which the plot of *Hawksmoor* develops. The novel is an astonishing *tour de force* that attempts to recreate the confused and contradictory intellectual atmosphere of the period of the Enlightenment from the double perspective of both its emergent empiricism, embodied in the novel by Sir Christopher Wren and the members of the Royal Society, and its strong undercurrent of submerged and repressed occult practices, represented by Wren's assistant architect, called Nicholas Dyer (instead of Nicholas Hawksmoor).

The coexistence of official empiricism and these subterranean magical practices is expressed in the novel through its all-encompassing duality. Structurally, duality is expressed in the combination of two apparently different stories: one, narrated in the odd-numbered chapters, covers the span of Nicholas Dyer's life: 1654–1715, which he recreates in a first-person narration supposedly written between 1711 and 1715, during the time he was employed to build the churches. In the even-numbered chapters, an external narrator reports the investigation carried out by a twentieth-century detective, Nicholas Hawksmoor, to solve a series of mysterious murders of boys and tramps recently committed near the seven (instead of the historical six) churches built by Dyer, which strikingly resemble those committed by the architect two centuries before.

Duality is expressed too in the fact that fictional characters existing in the eighteenth-century chapters reappear in those devoted to the twentieth century,[6] and also in the striking complementarity between Nicholas Hawksmoor and Nicholas Dyer. Their shared Christian names and the surname 'Dyer' already suggest the existence between them of a 'self/shadow' (or *Doppelgänger*) relationship, enhanced by the fact that both look alike, share the same thoughts, repeat similar acts, and seem to be undergoing a process of self-fragmentation and alienation from society.

At the same time, the reader also senses the strange communion of Dyer and Hawksmoor with the victims and tramps they respectively pursue or investigate. But the reverse holds too, for the victims also identify themselves with Dyer, and Hawksmoor is also sometimes associated with Sir Christopher Wren .... Indeed, as we go on reading, we find more and more shocking reduplications of names, events, actions and even identical sentences uttered by characters who live two centuries apart, until we are forced to conclude that, in the novel, nothing progresses in time, that the same events repeat themselves endlessly, and that the same people live and die only in order to be born and to live the same events again and again, eternally caught in the ever-revolving wheel of life and death. The same wheel Dyer recognizes with a pang in Sir Christopher Wren's experiment of the 'Moving Picture' (H. 141–2).

This interchangeability of characters and circularity of the events narrated is enhanced structurally by the device of using the same words to end and to begin adjacent chapters, and by the fact that the criss-crossing of references does not move, as one might expect, in a single direction, from the eighteenth to the twentieth century, but rather works forwards and backwards at the same time, disrupting traditional notions of chronological linearity in favour of a circular, or mythical conception of time.

This circular conception of time is in keeping with Nicholas Dyer's belief in the *Scientia Umbrarum*, an occult science developed out of neolithic, hermetic, cabbalistic and gnostic elements.[7] A most important aspect of Dyer's faith is the belief that Satan/Cain has authority over this world, and that, therefore, human life is a fall from grace. Dyer appears to be literally crushed by the weight of this awful knowledge and the conviction that he is condemned to eternal transmigration from body to body, unless in one life he manages to accomplish a Great Work comparable to God's act of creation of the cosmos. From this perspective, the episode in which the tramp called Ned identifies with the terrified black cat 'which was hurling itself in fear against one child and then another in order to break free, only to be caught and hauled back into the centre of the circle' (H. 81) becomes an apt proleptic icon of Dyer's attempt to escape the clutches of the planetary daemons that, he believes, prevent him from crossing the cosmic spheres and from achieving his transcendental assumption to the spiritual realm.

As a magician, Dyer strongly believes in the hermetic Principle of Correspondence, synthesized in the dictum 'as below, so above: as above, so below'. This principle, which may be considered the cornerstone of sympathetic magic, synthesizes the theory that man is the earthly counterpart of God and that events on earth parallel the doings of God in heaven. So, events in the sky are signals of events on earth, but the contrary also holds, that is, occurrences on earth are evidence of conditions in heaven. Consequently, the magician capable of manipulating events here 'below' can affect the course of events 'above'.[8] Therefore, by arranging his churches in a certain pattern that reproduces the pattern of the seven fixed stars in heaven through calculation of 'the positions and influences of the Celestial bodies and the Heavenly Orbs' (*H*. 5), Dyer is literally attempting to build a huge power-concentrating talisman capable of controlling the planetary spheres between heaven and earth, and thus hopes to submit to his will the seven planetary daemons who control them and prevent his transcendental ascesis. In other words, Dyer's huge 'septilateral pattern' – a Great Work comparable to the creation of a cosmos – is aimed at establishing a current of sympathetic magic between heaven and earth that would function as a magical ladder to heaven, or, in Dyer's own words, as 'an everlasting Order, which I may run through laughing: no one can catch me now' (*H*. 186).

From the time he disappeared in the crypt of Little St Hugh in 1715 until Detective Hawksmoor enters the church in the twentieth century, Dyer has undergone a series of split or *Doppelgänger* reincarnations both as victim and as murderer: each time he is reborn as child or tramp, the new child or tramp is subsequently murdered by his 'shadow' or dark emanation. In his last, twentieth-century reincarnation, his evil, or 'shadow' facet is embodied by the tramp called 'The Architect', his good or rational side by Nicholas Hawksmoor. So, after finishing the talismanic pattern of the churches, all that remains to be done is to reconcile these two opposed and split potentialities, the 'light' and the 'shadow', Dyer's divine and satanic facets, which must be brought into harmony in order for Dyer to achieve the new godlike totality of the Self.

The novel closes with the meeting of the tramp called 'The Architect' and detective Hawksmoor in Little St Hugh. As they come face to face in the darkness of the church, the two fuse into each other, forming a unity in the shadow their two figures cast upon the stone. Then they speak 'with one voice' (*H*. 217). And the text itself echoes their reunification: what they say is physically separated by a wide blank on the page, indicating a metalepsis, or change of narrative level. From the narrative point of view, then, the duality expressed in the alternation of narrative voices in the successive chapters is finally merged in a first-person narration uttered by somebody who is neither 'The Architect' nor Hawksmoor.

At the archetypal and mythical level there is no doubt that the one who speaks is the reunified Self, Dyer-as-Cosmic Man, the summation of 'The Architect' and Hawksmoor, ascending at last to the sphere of the stars 'on a winding path of smooth stones', the split, inferior selves remaining behind like the discarded fleshly garments in Plato's theory, as the last sentence of the first paragraph suggests: 'And when *I looked back*, they were watching one another silently' (*H.* 217, my emphasis). But we still don't know what the means are by which the twentieth-century detective manages to direct his steps to the transcendental meeting place where 'The Architect', his black emanation, is waiting for him. The answer is that he finds it, like the reader of Dante's *Divine Comedy*, by rightly interpreting Dyer's book.

At one point in his investigations, detective Hawksmoor received a strange old book with white covers and the remains of sealing wax on it that contains complex designs and puzzling explanations about the building of churches. This book is Nicholas Dyer's secret diary in which he has carefully annotated the 'laws of harmonious proportion' that rule the building of the pyramids, of obelisks and of megalithic circles, as well as of his churches. The day Dyer decided to destroy this book, it disappeared from his locked trunk only to reappear mysteriously in the hands of a tramp who tore it to pieces before it was anonymously sent to Hawksmoor. The detective also tore several pages of the book to stick them on the wall, in order to have the designs of the churches constantly in view. He studied these labyrinthine designs and suddenly realized that the connecting link between the churches was Nicholas Dyer, the architect who had built them two centuries before. It is then that he starts searching for a tramp nicknamed 'The Architect' and feels the impulse to go to Little St Hugh, where he eventually finds him.

At the beginning of his narration, Dyer, instructing his assistant Walter Pyne on the basics of transcendental architecture, compares architectural design with the writing of a book.

His comparison brings to mind the medieval Christian belief that God, the Cosmocrator, or Universal Architect, is the author of the Book of Nature. We may say, therefore, that Dyer's analogical activity is twofold: he has tried to recreate the (fiendish) Creator's cosmic plan in the geometrical figure cast by his churches but also, and most importantly, in the writing of his mysterious book which, we discover with amazement, may well be the very book that we have in our hands. This confers a strange transcendental quality to our own act of reading, for, if Dyer, like Dante, may achieve his transcendental transformation by the sheer act of writing himself into his book, the reader capable of truly interpreting Dyer's book may also achieve his/ her own essential transformation, as the reader of the *Divine Comedy* does, by analogically interpreting the book s/he is reading as the verbal construction reproducing Nicholas Dyer's cosmogonic pattern. In this sense, the fact that Little St Hugh is not a real Hawksmoor church, but rather the fictitious creation of Peter Ackroyd, acquires a new significance, for it only exists within the cardboard boundaries of Peter Ackroyd's fictional world. We also realize now that, beyond its literal interpretation, the distribution of the novel into twelve chapters hides a more profound analogical meaning for, like the twelve days of Epiphany, and the twelve months of the year, the twelve chapters prefigure a whole cosmogonic cycle whose beginning is clearly marked by the apocalyptic Great Fire with which the novel starts. So, the novel is suddenly revealed both as Borgesian 'Garden of Forking Paths', and as transcendental Jacob's ladder, or cabbalistic ladder of the Sephirot casting the reader upwards into eternity. From this perspective, the puzzling contradiction existing between Iain Sinclair's (and Spenser Spender's in *The Great Fire of London*) remark that the Hawksmoor churches form a 'pentacle star' and Dyer's insistence that he has constructed a 'septilateral figure' is also explained, for the missing pyramidal angle exists on a third, transcendental dimension, that of Plato's (and F. H. Bradley's) Sublime and Absolute Logos, but also in Borges's (and Oscar Wilde's) equally atemporal and absolute though simultaneously fictional and linguistic World of Art created by the power of Peter Ackroyd's imagination.

In 1989 Ackroyd published *First Light*, a novel that announced itself as 'a great leap away from the urban world of *Hawksmoor* and *Chatterton'*.[9] This description is accurate only literally, in the sense that the action of *First Light* does not take place in London, but rather in the rural south-west of England, in a fictional Pilgrin Valley situated on the Dorset–Devon border, near Lyme Regis and Axminster, which brings to mind the real Cheesecombe in Uplyme where Ackroyd used to spend his holidays between 1986 and 1990, and also recalls the area in far North Devon near Wales where Ackroyd owned Hannaford House, between 1990 and 1994. Ackroyd considers this area a very haunted part of England, and indeed it is a land full of mythical and literary echoes that shows its antiquity in the richness and variety of its fossils, of its prehistoric remains and of its autochthonous folklore. That is, although *First Light* is not situated in the mythical London of Ackroyd's earlier fiction, it is equally situated in a mythical land whose origins go back to the very dawn of civilization. Moreover, the new novel shows the same overriding concern with time, with the constructedness of reality and with the myth of origins that obsessed Philip Slack and other 'humanist' characters in Ackroyd's earlier fiction.

Structurally, *First Light* may be described as a multiplot novel that combines three main narrative lines. The first one develops around the discovery of an ancient tumulus in Pilgrin Valley and the ensuing excavations carried out by a team directed by the archaeologist Mark Clare with the muted opposition of the local owners of the surrounding land, Farmer and Boy Mint. The second one is about the arrival at the valley of a retired music-hall comedian, Joey Hanover and his wife Floey, in search of the parents and home he lost at the age of 5. The third narrative line centres on the observation of the stars carried out by the astronomer Damian Fall in Holblack Moor Observatory. An external omniscient narrator alternates the narration of these originally unrelated narrative lines, progressively knitting an intricate net of relationships that will eventually materialize in the establishment of their mutual connection and interdependence. Embedded within the first narrative level, there is also a series of tales and visions (as happened in *The Last Testament of Oscar Wilde*), told by several internal narrators–characters that function as overtly 'literary' variations on different episodes narrated in one of the main narrative lines or on the novel as a whole (like the tales in *The Last Testament*).

49

Although the protagonists of the three narrative lines had never met before they arrived at Pilgrin Valley and although they are apparently pursuing their own particular goals, in fact they are equally obsessed with the myth of origins, which they try to verify at three complementary ontological levels: Mark Clare looks down into the bowels of the earth, cutting across geological layers in an attempt to reach the original prehistoric culture that flourished in the area at the very origin of humankind; Damian Fall looks up into the sky and studies the movements of the stars as a way to reach back to the Big Bang, that is, the 'first light', the atemporal moment of the creation of the cosmos (*FL* 262). And Joey Hanover roams the surface of the valley in an attempt to establish his own origins through the recuperation of his lost family line and place of birth. However, having forgotten the hermetic principle: 'as below, so above; as above, so below', none of them realizes at the start that their respective quests for origins are complementary, that the past of the earth, of humankind and of the stars are all interrelated manifestations of the unitary cosmos.

During his life on earth, 'Old Barren One', the magician buried in the tumulus, had tried – like Nicholas Dyer – to apply his knowledge to control the influence of Aldebaran, the largest star in the Pleiades and 'the star which controlled all the sighs and tears of the earth' (*FL* 295). When the forest fire revealed the existence of the tumulus to the archaeologists, they could not understand why it was on the edge of an area marked by stones forming 'an ellipse more than a mile in circumference, so that the actual centre lies over the valley' (*FL* 239). That is, they failed to realize that the dome-shaped tumulus, encircled by long wooden poles 'which had all been burnt at the same time [representing] a ritual conflagration after the tomb had been sealed' (*FL* 137), was imitating the position of a planet or fixed star describing a parabolic curve on its course around the sun. The star the tumulus replicates is Aldebaran, as the phonetic closeness of the star's and the magician's names suggests. In other words, the valley encircled in the ellipse (like Dyer's septilateral figure) is a man-made cosmos, the magician's talismanic replica of the Pleiades. By building it and burying himself in the tumulus, Old Barren, like Dyer, was hoping to achieve his transcendental 'change' from man to *anthropos*, the

Cosmic Man in Vitrubius's theory that Leonardo da Vinci drew as a Star Man with arms and legs outstretched. Still, making good the hermetic formula 'as below, so above; as above, so below', the magician's reproduction of the stars also works the other way, for, as Damian Fall is astonished to observe, Aldebaran itself 'has taken on the shape of Pilgrin Valley' (FL 155).

The Star Man's creation of this unitary cosmos caused time to stand still: life in the valley seems to follow an unchangeable pattern of birth, reproduction and death, a situation that comes to an end when the tumulus is unearthed and systematically destroyed by the archaeologists, with the consequence that the harmonious knot of sympathetic magic that had kept the balance between good and evil, Cosmos and Chaos, for over 4,000 years comes to an end. Fittingly, the disruption of this balance in the valley is experienced by Damian Fall as 'the death of the cosmos' (FL 296). After Old Barren One is removed from the tumulus, Fall is astonished to discover that Aldebaran, 'the dying star', had reversed its course and 'was now moving towards the earth. It was approaching at enormous speed' (FL 293, 295).

Other characters also witness the strange phenomena caused by the destruction of the tumulus. When, incapable of protecting Old Barren One from the archaeologists, the Mints eventually decide to set fire to the coffin, Joey Hanover has an experience of temporal disruption – 'Time turning'. Watching the body, he is transported backwards, to the time when the wise man died. And he has a vision of the Star Man 'touch[ing] hands with the one before him, and touch[ing] hands with the one who follows', that echoes the vision of Chatterton, Meredith and Wychwood with joined hands at the end of Chatterton. Then (in a scene that recalls Clement Harcombe's face taking on the lineaments of the faces of the Harcombes 'stretch[ing] back to the beginning' in English Music), when the flames reduce the wise man's fleshly garment to ashes, Joey 'sees in this face, too, the faces of all those who had come before him. And the faces of all those he has known. This is the human face he recognised in all those he has loved' (FL 321–3).

For the Mints it is clear that the spirit of the Star Man 'had been released at last. He had returned to the frame of origins'

51

(*FL* 326). However, the release of the Star Man's spirit also means the release of his hold on the evil forces of Chaos which he had kept buried 'beneath'. Damian Fall acutely senses this evil flowing into the old cottage, where he has a growing feeling that he is 'surrounded by some inexplicable and unfathomable horror' (*FL* 177). The cottage has behind it a tragic history of death and suicide associated with witchcraft. Fall has described it as another tumulus, and the cottage, with its carved Star Men and its encircling high hedge of fire-like 'purple flowers' (*FL* 148), may be seen as representing the intermediate or 'earthly' point of intersection between the 'heavenly' observatory and the 'hellish' tumulus towards which both Aldebaran and Old Barren now converge, for it is on this intermediate ontological level that the forces of Light and Darkness must fight a new battle for pre-eminence. And it is here, of course, that they find Damian Fall, the astronomer, the only man capable of restoring harmony to the valley, by the repetition of a new ritual act of creation of the cosmos.

At the beginning of the novel, we saw Damian Fall at Holblack Moor Observatory talking to his assistant Alec about the origins of the universe and equating the New Physics to 'the first myth' (*FL* 4). Echoing the circularity of mythical time, the novel, with neat symmetry, ends with the same speech, although Damian Fall, who is now in bed – perhaps in a mental asylum – is addressing the same speech to his own 'shadow', which he identifies with Aldebaran (*FL* 327). At this stage, the reader also realizes that the identification of Aldebaran with Damian Fall was already inscribed in the surname 'Fall', which prefigures the 'fall' of Aldebaran from its sphere. This identity is also suggested when, watching the fall of 'the red giant' in the computer, Damian 'caught his own face reflected in that screen, bathed in red with the mouth and eyes quite dark' (*FL* 296–7). In other words, the novel ends leaving Fall in the position of the various visionary characters in earlier fiction considered to be mad by their contemporaries, whereas in fact he is the only one who 'knows' the new astronomer the Star Man has chosen to transmit his knowledge to, or, to put it differently, to reincarnate himself in; Damian Fall is, therefore, the new Star Man on whose shoulders rests the responsibility of restoring the lost harmony between Man and Cosmos, but he is also the Fool on whose shoulders rest the pain and sorrow of the world, as Evangeline Tupper (the civil servant from the Department of the Environment) intuits – 'Someone is playing the fool' (*FL* 124) –, a Christ figure, as he himself realizes (*FL* 177), who, like Dyer, must be both propitiatory victim and murderer, hanged man and magus; that is, must know the depths of utter good and evil. And, although the task appals him at the start, Damian Fall seems eventually to accept his fate, as he is not afraid of his shadow any more, but rather 'smiled' at it (*FL* 327).

According to mythical thought, the expulsion from paradise and his ensuing loss of contact with the divinity reduces man to a single plane of existence: his human nature. This is the state in which Damian Fall finds himself at the beginning of the novel. Reduced to his human nature, Fall cannot conceive of other planes of existence. Therefore, when he discovers the many coincidences between the findings of the New Physics and the postulates of myth, he is panic-stricken with the realization that 'there were no stars, *there were only words* with which we choose to decorate the sky' (*FL* 297, my emphasis). His fear of non-being is like the *Angst* of the Beckettian hero, confronted with the belief that he cannot transcend the prison-house of his own mind, that there is an unbridgeable gap between the world and its – linguistic or mathematical – human representations. Therefore, for Damian, the only solution is to accept Blake's contention that the human imagination has a transcendental capacity, that the human representations of reality are true. This is the lesson Chatterton transmitted to Charles Wychwood and this is indeed the secret carefully kept by the Mints that had allowed Old Barren to transcend his human condition and become a Star Man.

It is only within this transcendental logic that the many metafictional and intertextual allusions that suffuse the novel acquire their true dimension: they are not realism-undermining mechanisms but, on the contrary, the very guarantee of the novel's truthfulness and reality. Within this logic, it is easy to understand why the description of Pilgrin Valley with its subterranean caves and river and its dome-like tumulus follows so closely Coleridge's famous description of Kubla Khan's palace in Xanadu; and why the characters themselves are likewise built on the accumulation of literary echoes. Mark Clare, for example, with his 'long sideburns which covered half of his cheeks' and his 'green deerstalker hat' (FL 8, 6) is a parodic crossbreed of Sherlock Holmes and Dr Watson. But his personality is further complicated by his allusive surname 'Clare', which he owes to Thomas Hardy's character Angel Clare, from *Tess of the D'Urbervilles*. Moreover, he has a dog called Jude, like the timorous Hardy protagonist. And, where Farmer Lodge's wife, in Hardy's short story has 'a withered arm' that leads her to a tragic death, Mark Clare's wife Kathleen has a 'withered leg' that is the cause of her overwhelming fits of depression and eventual suicide.

Likewise, the Mints, the rural people who supported the wise men and kept their wisdom alive in their popular songs and ballads, share basic traits in common with Hardy's 'folk'. However, for all their apparent garrulousness and rustic simplicity, they do not look like peasants, but clowns. Farmer Mint with 'his usual collection of heterogeneous garments [and] old flat cap' and his hair 'sprouting from all over his face and head', stands for the 'silly' clown, while Boy Mint with his almost complete hairlessness and his puzzling witticisms stands for the 'clever' clown (FL 19). Indeed, their behaviour is so suspect that, after talking with them, Mark considers the possibility that Farmer and Boy Mint 'had been putting on an act, that they had been performing for his benefit' (FL 21). Their clownishness and their inborn acting capacity has been inherited by the last Mint, Joey Hanover, the retired music-hall and television star who had come to the region with his wife Floey, an ex-music-hall dancer, in search of his lost parents. As their artistic names suggest 'Joey and Floey' share the Punch and Judy clownishness that forms such an intrinsic part of Harriet Scrope's and of Mr and Mrs Leno's personalities in *Chatterton*, and Joey's persona is literally described by the narrator as 'close to that of Dan Leno or Max Miller' (FL 68). In other words, Joey Mint is a 'monopolylinguist', the representative of what Ackroyd considers to be a specifically English sensibility. In this sense, his increasing inability to remember the lines of the songs that intersperse his speech (like Floey's ludicrous malapropisms) is a clear symptom of the diminished condition of the ancient culture he represents.

Other characters and episodes are intertextually connected to

Hardy's Wessex novels and short stories. But to say that Hardy provides the only intertexts of *First Light* would be totally misleading. The novel is also perceptibly suffused with echoes of Jane Austen, T. S. Eliot, Joyce, Fowles, Blake, Dickens, Frazer, Kipling, Melville, Sheridan, Dylan Thomas, Voltaire and Wilde, as well as with echoes of Ackroyd's own earlier fiction. Indeed, the list of intertextual references could be extended *ad infinitum*, for *First Light* is a Borgesian Library of Babel, a derivative and self-conscious textual world peopled by cardboard characters, capable however of dreaming themselves into immortality by virtue of Peter Ackroyd's magus-like act of imaginative creation. A novel, that is, written to demonstrate in practice the wrongness of Sir James G. Frazer's statement in *The Golden Bough*, reproduced in the epigraph to Part Six, that 'all magic is necessarily false and barren' (*FL* 291).

Ackroyd's next novel, *The House of Doctor Dee* (1993), shares with *Hawksmoor* and *First Light* the same conception of myth. The novel begins when the contemporary narrator–character, Matthew Palmer, inherits from his father an old house in Clerkenwell that had belonged to Doctor John Dee, the most famous magician in London during the reign of Elizabeth I. The house of Doctor Dee, like the churches built by Nicholas Dyer in *Hawksmoor*, or like the prehistoric tumulus unearthed in the Dorset countryside in *First Light*, or like the Marshalsea Prison in *The Great Fire of London*, still holds the concentrated power of its earlier inhabitants. When Matthew Palmer moves into the house, he experiences a series of uncanny events; as a result his character is altered, his sensual drives heightened, and he is seized by an obsessive desire to know more details about its earlier owner.

Following the pattern established in *Hawksmoor*, *The House of Doctor Dee* alternates two stories and periods: one told by Matthew Palmer is set in 1993 (*HDD* 219), the year of publication of the novel; the other, narrated by Doctor John Dee, is set in the sixteenth century. The alternation of Matthew's and Doctor Dee's accounts is structurally enhanced by the fact that only Matthew's chapters are numbered – from 'ONE' to 'SEVEN' – while Doctor Dee's chapters, eight in number, simply have chapter-headings. To these a last, atemporal chapter is added, 'THE VISION', narrated by the combined voices of Matthew

55

Palmer, John Dee and Peter Ackroyd that brings to mind the merging of narrative voices at the end of *Hawksmoor*.

After inheriting the house, Matthew becomes obsessed with learning about its Renaissance owner. Interestingly, the further he seems to be travelling backwards in the course of his investigation, the further Doctor Dee seems to be travelling forward into the future. From the start, Matthew feels Dee's spirit suffusing the house and invading his dreams and he even hears his voice in the 'sealed up' chamber talking with his assistant, Edward Kelley (*HDD* 229), while, conversely, Doctor Dee also hears fragments of Matthew's conversation with his friend Daniel Moore in the 'scrying room' (*HDD* 188). Moreover, the reader often has the puzzling feeling that Matthew and Doctor Dee are involved in similar actions or episodes and seem to have striking biographical traits in common.

The historical Doctor Dee learnt natural magic and built automata during his university years at Cambridge. But, like his fictional *alter ego*, he was soon to abandon this practice in favour of the Cabbala which, in contrast to natural magic, seeks to raise the magician above the natural powers of the cosmos and aspires to achieve God's creative capacity. In the Jewish magical and mystical traditions, the creation is conceived as a code that can be deciphered and reproduced. The historical Doctor Dee applied these principles in his most influential book, the *Monas Hieroglyphica* (1564), where he represents the complex unity and wholeness of Man (Man as microcosm) with the symbol of the 'hieroglyphic monad'. This symbol combines the *ternarivs* (body, soul and spirit) with the *quaternarivs* (the four basic elements: earth, air, water and fire), to form a *septenarivs* which hides the most secret *octonarivs*, the overall symbol of the complex unity of the monad, what the alchemists called the 'philosopher's stone'. Dee represents the hieroglyphic monad diagrammatically as follows:[10]

Like Nicholas Dyer and Old Barren One, John Dee believed that man can aspire to a spiritual transmutation or essential change by means of ascesis that would remove him from the world of matter to the world of the spirit. However, as an alchemist, Dee believes that this change can only be induced by the separation (or 'decoding') of the four basic constitutive elements (often symbolized by colours), with the help of what he calls 'igneous art', mentioned by one of the spirits who speaks with Kelley in the novel as '*Ignis vera mater*' (*HDD* 202). The alchemic separation of these elements could also be used for the creation of an artificial man, what the fifteenth-century physician Paracelsus called a *homunculus* (or, in cabbalistic terms, a *golem*), as is suggested by Dee's vision of 'the creature that is born twice, crying out upon the top of a mountain and saying, "I am the white of the black, and the red of the white, and the yellow of the sun, I tell truth and lie not"' (*HDD* 51).

During his life on earth, the fictional Doctor Dee undertakes two main tasks. The first one is 'to find our forefathers', 'the race before the Flood [who were] not giants of physical but of spiritual power' (*HDD* 190–1). This task brings to mind the prehistoric culture that built the tumulus in *First Light* and recalls William Blake's belief in the existence of 'a giant race which had been dispersed over the globe, bearing with it memorials of an ancient faith',[11] and also the myth of the lost continent of Atlantis, (*HDD* 66, 155 and *passim*) of which the British Isles were considered to be the only remnant. As Dee explains to Edward Kelley, the city is 'more than three thousand years before our present age, when there was such power upon the earth that all men were like gods', and it is clear that the city Doctor Dee has in mind, like Blake's Albion, and Bacon's New Atlantis, is a mystical city, 'formed within the spiritual body of man', for, in common with 'Pico della Mirandola and Hermes Trismegistus', Dee believes that self and world are one and the same (*HDD* 190, 273, 68).

The second task is related to the first. It consists in discovering 'the divinity within, that soul, that spark, that fire which drives the spheres' (*HDD* 104), that is, the discovery of the *spiritus mundi*, God's creative spark existing in all things (*HDD* 77). The search for this unitary and essential substance (named by the alchemists the 'philosopher's stone') is what had driven the covetous crook Edward Kelley to offer himself as Doctor Dee's assistant and 'scryer'. Dee himself was at first very interested in minting gold, and his obsession with material wealth was such that he even abandoned his father on his deathbed in order to search for a supposed buried treasure (*HDD* 102). However, he soon understands the fruitlessness of this pursuit and abandons it in favour of the spiritual aspect of alchemy, which, we must not forget, is the art of 'mint[ing] gold both material and spiritual'. Henceforth Dee will concentrate his effort on the task of creating 'new life without the help of any womb [...] an everlasting creature' (*HDD* 189, 104).

After moving into the house, Matthew finds in Doctor Dee's study a glass tube that later disappears and is replaced by some sheets of paper with 'DOCTOR DEE'S RECIPE' for the creation of a *homunculus* (*HDD* 123). His gardener also finds 'a ring of bones' at the bottom of 'a small pit' in the garden, which might belong to a dead dog or cat, but which, to Matthew's imagination, seems 'the remains of a child' (*HDD* 122). At the same time, Matthew is troubled by his incapacity to recall anything about his early childhood (*HDD* 174, 176), and the more he learns about his father's involvement with Doctor Dee's magical practices, the more he puzzles about the question of his origins. Therefore, when his mother tells him that he was adopted, her words haunt Matthew and the reader alike with the disturbing possibility that Doctor Dee's experiment may have been successful and that Matthew, the 29-year-old narrator, may in fact be a *homunculus*, who 'will grow and prosper until its thirtieth year when it will fall asleep and return to its first unformed state' (*HDD* 123) in order to be reborn again.

The historical Doctor Dee believed that angels and demons existed on a different dimension but that it was possible to get into contact with them in specific spaces which functioned as 'doors'. He believed that one such geographic space was Glastonbury, the ancient borough in Somerset associated with King Arthur and the Holy Grail, where Doctor Dee is supposed to have searched for the Elixir. Another was Greenland, known then as the land of Thule. In the novel, Dee and Kelley search for such a place in Glastonbury, 'the most ancient seat of learning in the entire kingdom, where, it is said, the giants who originally inhabited this realm had placed their secrets' (*HDD* 145). They

58

also look for the site of the ancient city of London in the Wapping marshes (where Matthew's father owns a garage). Another example of a connecting 'door' between different dimensions is the 'small globe of clear glass' (*HDD* 165) they use to propitiate the passage of the angelic beings from the spiritual world to that of matter. Yet another is the 'sealed up' door in the basement of Doctor Dee's house that, nevertheless, sometimes opens of its own accord (*HDD* 14). But it may be said that Doctor Dee's house as a whole is a huge transdimensional door, as suggested by Matthew's uncanny experiences in it and by his vision of himself entering the house for the first time and opening four different doors:

> It had four doors, the first of which was black, the second as white and as transparent as crystal, the third was green, and the fourth red. I opened the first door, and the house was full of black dust like gunpowder. I opened the white door, and the rooms within were pale and empty. I opened the third door, and there appeared a cloud of water as if the house were – a fountain. Then I opened the fourth door, and I saw a furnace. (*HDD* 9–10)

The black, white, green and red colours of the doors are the alchemic colours of the *quaternarivs*, that is, of the four basic constitutive elements: earth ('dust'); air ('pale and empty'); water ('cloud' and 'fountain'); and fire ('furnace'). As we have seen, the spiritual transmutation of man can only be achieved through the separation of these elements, and the house, which is literally 'descending into ground' (*HDD* 5), has three storeys at underground, ground and above-ground levels that may be said to replicate the *ternarivs* or cosmic levels, and also their human equivalents, body, soul and spirit. This equation is explicitly made by Matthew when he states that the central section 'resembled the torso of a man rearing up, while his arms still lay spread upon the ground on either side [...] it was as if I were about to enter a human body' (*HDD* 3).

We may conclude, therefore, that the house, shaped like a human body with outstretched arms is a striking example of the *monas hieroglyphica*, the materialization of Doctor Dee as Cosmic Man or *anthropos*. In this light, Matthew's offhand remark that 'I was becoming part of the old house' (*HDD* 44), enhances the suggested *Doppelgänger* relationship between Matthew and Dee, while, from a Swedenborgian perspective, it refers to his belonging to Doctor Dee's 'spiritual family'.

But the house is much older than Doctor Dee. As Matthew noted, it 'was not of any one period'. It is situated at the geographic centre of London; on the site of a 'medieval brothel [...] just beyond the nunnery', that is, at the crossroads of good and evil; and also near the medieval 'Clerks' Well', considered to be an emblem of 'spiritual blessing' (HDD 1, 2, 17, 16). The centrality of the place, then, its dual good/evil nature and its association with regenerative water, as well as its three-storey structure confirms the house's condition of *umbilicus/axis mundi*, that is, of being the navel/centre of the world.

In this light, the symbolic correspondences between Doctor Dee's house and the 'lost and ancient city of London' is striking. In the chapter entitled 'THE CHAMBER OF DEMONSTRATION' an angelic being describes this city along the same lines: 'there are four natural keys to open five gates of the city (for one gate is never to be opened), and by their means will the secret of this place be righteously and wisely granted to you' (HDD 193). In other words, Doctor Dee's house is both the microcosmic replica of 'London eternal' and its centre (as the three 'houses' in *First Light* are the centre and replica of Pilgrin Valley). But we should not forget that the house is also a hieroglyphic monad, the emblem of Cosmic Man, and that the mystical city of London only exists within the 'spiritual body' of the English, so that the house is also the navel of the Cosmic Body of the English race at large, a condition made evident by the fact that since Doctor Dee's death the house has always been inhabited by 'visionary' craftsmen associated with London radicalism.

After the arrival of Kelley, Doctor Dee's progress in his occult knowledge improves dramatically. However, this does not seem to increase his happiness or spiritual bliss. In fact, the more he trusts Edward Kelley and the spirits raised by cabbalistic means, the more unjust and unloving he becomes, making the members of his household unhappy. It is at this point that two family ghosts will help him to re-evaluate his art by means of two complementary visions: 'THE CITY' and 'THE GARDEN'.

Doctor Dee's father had died in 'an alms-house and hospital for the aged' (HDD 94), neglected and unloved by his son. Consequently, it is the ghost of his father who offers John Dee the fearful vision of 'THE CITY', or of what he calls 'the world without love'. In this vision, human beings appear as Eliotean 'hollow men'; love becomes *amor sexus*, and London acquires 'the image of a man mounting a woman and coupling with her in a rape'. It is a city of 'sorrow', 'separation' and 'darkness', a world of corruption and sickness in which Doctor Dee, condemned to death for the poisoning of his wife, witnesses his own hanging and, in a subverted version of his transcendental ascesis, walks down the 'new stairs' by Watergate that would take him to the barge where a Charon who looks exactly like himself will carry him to hell (*HDD* 203–11). Hell itself is presided over by Elizabeth I, who tears to pieces and greedily consumes a naked corpse that is both Doctor Dee's body and that of England (*HDD* 215–16), in a plastic image of the cause–effect relationship existing between Man's evil actions and the death of his Spiritual Body. Moreover, Dee's lovelessness seems to have set a recurrent pattern. Matthew's father also seems to have been fatally influenced by Dee's evil practices and to have projected his lovelessness onto Matthew, for, as he reflects, 'I had grown up in a world without love, a world of magic, of money, of possession, and so I had none for myself or for others' (*HDD* 178).

Doctor Dee was so deceived and misled by Edward Kelley that it is only after his wife Katherine dies that he truly understands the extent of his blindness. In a deathbed scene suffused with romantic echoes, Katherine promises to return after her death, in order to show her husband a different road to wisdom, not the 'total' knowledge of the cabbalist that creates *homunculi* and a world without love, but rather the *docta ignorantia* of the hermetic magus and of the radical craftsman. In 'THE GARDEN' we share with Doctor Dee the vision of this world. The separation, darkness and suffering of 'THE CITY' have given way to the beautiful and placid vision of 'the philosopher's garden, which is normally closed with such locks and bars that no one may enter' (*HDD* 247). In this lovely *hortus conclusus* John Dee sees his mother/wife pregnant with 'a man child' who, like Doña Inés for Don Juan Tenorio, has offered her soul to God as pawn for his sins (*HDD* 245, 251). It is in the light of this perfectly unselfish motherly/wifely love that Doctor Dee is allowed to contemplate the 'spirit of beauty' burning 'with a quenchless flame, like a blazing beacon, or like a sparkling torch' within the flowers, and 'men and women set for dancing' – like Eliot's peasants in 'Burnt Norton'[12] – each one with his mate, 'the humane beings who have taken the true path of life'. He then saw that these men and women formed 'a pattern of people in perfect order and symmetry', and realized in amazement that 'the star man' he had always sought to create was within himself (HDD 252–6).

After this vision of 'the world of love', Doctor Dee, in a Prospero-like gesture,[13] abjures his art and his search for the homunculus and realizes, like earlier Ackroydian characters, that 'There is no way to conquer time and live eternally except through vision. The vision, not the body, transcends this life' (HDD 270).

Almost simultaneously with this revelation, Matthew Palmer undergoes a similar numinous experience. Just as Doctor Dee was saved by the love of his wife, so Matthew's spiritual barrenness is overcome with the help of his mother, whose closeness to the 'world of love' is symbolized by the splendid sunflowers growing in her garden (HDD 178–9) (like those of Clement Harcombe in English Music).

In his Testament, Doctor Dee had cryptically said that he left a stone 'for those that may find it' (HDD 227). Matthew will eventually find this stone in the small locked-up garage his father had in Wapping. When he looks at it, he sees 'a large piece of stone [that] seemed to emit a vague glow' but really was 'patches of moss and lichen which spread across its surface' (HDD 263). On closer scrutiny he notices that the stone has the form of three steps – like the stairs Dee had gone down to take Charon's barge in his vision of hell, but also like the steps that lead down to the sealed door in Doctor Dee's house. In the garage, however, the steps lead nowhere and make Matthew realize that 'up and down are the same here'. This apparently banal realization synthesizes, however, the core of hermeticism, the belief that the way to hell and heaven is one and the same. Climbing up them Matthew feels dizzy, and climbing down them 'had so strong a sensation of vertigo that I might have been descending miles into the earth' (HDD 264). Indeed, it seems that Matthew has finally found the octonarivs itself, the most secret, overall symbol of the hieroglyphic monad, the very transdimensional 'door' of the mythical city of London left by

Doctor Dee 'for those that may find it' in his *Testament*, which he rubricated with the sentence: 'Follow my footsteps beyond the grave' (*HDD* 226).

It is after this uncanny experience that Matthew, on his return to the Clerkenwell house, unexpectedly encounters 'an unformed creature perched upon the gate' and realizes that: 'There never was a homunculus', that it was only 'a figment and a sick man's dream [...] the fantasy of those who believe in the reality of time and the power of the material world' (*HDD* 266).

Once Matthew decides to follow Dee's 'steps' and get rid of the shackles of the material world, the spatio-temporal barriers collapse, 'the veil' (*HDD* 6) is torn and the sixteenth- and the twentieth-century characters can meet at last in the transdimensional realm of the imagination. The city that opens its gates to Dee and Matthew is a beautiful, harmonious and holy city, where 'time never was' and 'is formed within the spiritual body of man'. It is in this spiritual city/body, built by Doctor Dee's passionate love, that he is met by his dead father and wife who 'took me by the hand and greeted me' (*HDD* 272–3). But it is also here that he will encounter Matthew Palmer and Peter Ackroyd himself, together with 'the Moravians of Arrow Lane, the Ranters, the followers of Jakob Boehme [...] Mary, in her leather coat; Nathaniel Cadman; Margaret Lucas; Daniel Moore; Katherine Dee; and so many others, all of them living within the city' (*HDD* 276). That is, he will encounter here the real and the fictional human beings who share the same imaginative vision of the world, for, as Swedenborg taught, 'each of us goes to a house, and to a family – not the same ones we possessed on earth, not them at all, but to the house and the family that correspond to our ruling passions. Whatever we wished for on earth we shall find after death' (*HDD* 90).

As in earlier novels, linear temporality gives way to circularity in the last chapter of *The House of Doctor Dee*: a conversation between Matthew and Daniel that had taken place in chapter 'ONE' 'About a year ago' is repeated and situated again 'About a year ago' in 'THE VISION'. In this conversation, Matthew is telling Daniel Moore about the vision he had had of 'a bridge of light [...] connecting two shores' (*HDD* 17–18, 273). On this bridge, he simultaneously meets the adult Doctor Dee and sees their shared pregnant mother/wife announcing Doctor Dee's rein-

63

carnation in himself, while at the same time we hear the voice of Peter Ackroyd, merging with that of Dee/Matthew, worrying about the historical accuracy of his recreation of the sixteenth-century magician. Indeed, in the bright world of the imagination opened up by this bridge, Matthew/Dee/Ackroyd can lose their individuality and join their voices (like Chatterton, Wychwood and Meredith, or Tim and Clement Harcombe) in the mystic union of Man's spiritual body, which 'exists eternally' (*HDD* 274–6).

The novel closes with Ackroyd's exhortation to Dee to 'become one with him' and help him to 'create another bridge across two shores'. With Ackroyd's exhortation in mind it is tempting to compare Ackroyd's task as a creator of fictional worlds with John Dee's task as the creator of a cosmos. And if we compare the novel with John Dee's *monas hieroglyphica*, we will be surprised by the neatness of the structural correspondences between the monad's constitutive elements and the chapter distribution, which, as in earlier novels, echoes the thematic connection between the chapters reported by Matthew Palmer and those narrated by Doctor Dee by the device of repeating the closing sentence of one chapter as the opening sentence of the next. Schematically the sequence would be as follows:

ONE > *<THE SPECTACLE >* < **TWO** > *<THE LIBRARY >*
*< **THREE** > <THE HOSPITAL > <* **FOUR**>*< THE ABBEY >*
*<***FIVE**>
[THE CHAMBER OF DEMONSTRATION} {THE CITY}]
< **SIX** >
[{THE CLOSET} {THE GARDEN]
< **SEVEN**>
[THE VISION]

The division of the first eight chapters into four pairs alternating the voices of Matthew and Dee can be said to correspond to the arrangement of the four elements of the *quaternarivs* in the hieroglyphic monad. The intertwining of chapters 'FIVE', 'SIX' and 'SEVEN' may be said to correspond to the three elements of the *ternarivs*, which, combined with the four last chapters narrated by Dee ('THE CHAMBER OF DEMONSTRATION', 'THE CITY', 'THE CLOSET' and 'THE GARDEN') form a *septenarivs*, leading to the last, transdimensional and atemporal chapter, 'THE VISION', which, like Dee's *octonarivs*, is 'most secret' and difficult to fathom, as it only exists within the 'spiritual body' created by Matthew/Dee/Ackroyd in conjunction with the earlier visionary writers and characters in the English tradition.

Thus, making good the Behemites' belief that 'the universe itself was in the shape of a single person' (*HDD* 45), *The House of Doctor Dee* shows its hidden condition of hieroglyphic monad, and reveals itself as a two-dimensional, yet infinite World/Book, the materialization of the spiritual body of a series of living creatures who can be seen either as *homunculi* or as *anthropoi*, as literary characters or as historical figures, for, like the mythical City/Book they inhabit and jointly beget, their nature strictly depends on the reader's capacity to find and follow the steps left by Matthew/Dee/Ackroyd 'for those that might find [them]'.

4

The Badness Will Pass in Time

The action of Ackroyd's next novel, *Dan Leno and the Limehouse Golem* (1994), shares significant traits with *The House of Doctor Dee*: it is situated in London's East End, the name of one of the main characters, John Cree, is phonetically close to John Dee, and it is about a 'golem', the Jewish equivalent of Doctor Dee's *homunculus*. Described by Peter Keating as 'a modern pastiche of the Victorian Shilling Shocker',[1] it develops, like *Hawksmoor*, around a series of ritual murders.

The novel is presented as the report of an anonymous twentieth-century narrator–historian who has been gathering material about two sets of murders committed in Limehouse in 1880: one is a 'private' and 'domestic' case – that is, typically Victorian, according to Gissing (*DLLG* 36): Elizabeth Cree's poisoning of her husband, an ex-newspaper reporter with a passion for the music hall and fascinated 'by poverty, and by the crime and disease which it engendered' (*DLLG* 44). The other, the 'shocking' and 'public' massacres of several representatives of the 'margins' of Victorian society: two prostitutes, a Jewish scholar, and a family of second-hand clothiers, attributed by the press to an invisible 'Limehouse Golem'.

The narrator, in, apparently, a desire for historical accuracy, reproduces extracts from the trial of Elizabeth Cree; and also extracts taken from the diary of Mr John Cree in which he attributes the Golem murders to himself. Interspersed with these 'historical' records are also some chapters in which Elizabeth Cree retrospectively narrates her life story. In this account, she confesses a whole new set of undetected murders that run parallel to the stages of her own transformation from poor and illegitimate child to music-hall comedian, respectable married woman, bad playwright, and Limehouse Golem.

In the chapters narrated by the twentieth-century external narrator, the account of the events includes the reactions and commentaries on the murders of a series of historical characters who live in the area, such as Karl Marx and George Gissing, who, like Dan Leno, Oscar Wilde and Bernard Shaw, often sit next to each other in the Reading Room of the British Museum. The attraction these historical characters (and also fictional characters such as Solomon Weil, and Elizabeth and John Cree) feel for the British Library is explained by the narrator as evidence that for many a Londoner 'the Reading Room was the true spiritual centre of London where many secrets might finally be revealed' (*DLLG* 269). This idea, also expressed by Ackroyd in 'London Luminaries and Cockney Visionaries',[2] brings to mind Iain Sinclair's belief that the Hawksmoor churches (see chapter 3), the British Museum and Greenwich Observatory are sources of occult power.

After meeting by chance in the Reading Room, Karl Marx and Solomon Weil develop a friendship based precisely on the very disparateness (or rather, complementarity) of their world-views. The materialist atheist and the cabbalistic magician soon find that they have a similar Jewish German background, 'a similar interest in theoretical enquiry and subtle disputes of learning', and also, implausibly, that they have been born 'in the same month and year' (*DLLG* 63). Indeed, as the German pronunciation of the 'w' in Weil (i.e. like an English 'v', recalling the word 'veil') suggests, Marx and Weil may be said to stand in a *Doppelgänger* or self/shadow relationship, an explanation that would be in keeping with the belief of a Cracowian sect of Jewish Gnostics mentioned by Weil that 'The malevolent spirits of the lower air could sometimes divide a departing soul into two or three "flames" or "flashes", so that the elements of the same person might be distributed into more than one body of the newly born' (*DLLG* 95).

Weil mentions this sect in the course of a conversation which had started with a discussion of the 'Golem'. For the cabbalist, the ancient legend should be taken allegorically, as 'an emblem' of degraded matter (*DLLG* 68). For Weil (as for Doctor Dee), the shape of the material world necessarily takes the form the human spirit gives it. This notion is essential for an understanding of the novel, for if the homunculus was the microcosmic evil emanation of Doctor Dee's house and 'a figment and a sick man's dream')[3], the Limehouse Golem may likewise be described as the macrocosmic evil emanation of the whole area of Limehouse and a figment of the sick Londoners' dream of greed and abysmal poverty brought about by the Industrial Revolution.

The murders of Jane Quig, Solomon Weil and Alice Stanton are performed according to a ritual reminiscent of the Ripper murders of prostitutes that historically took place during the 'Autumn of Terror' of the year 1888 in Whitechapel, that poverty-stricken area of East-End London that E. W. G. Chick has called 'the evil quarter mile'.[4]

In his contribution to *Who Was Jack the Ripper?*, Iain Sinclair refuses to speculate on the identity of the murderer and quotes the satanist Aleister Crowley, who contends that:

> the topography of the Whitechapel murders spells out a magical formula, conferring 'the gift of invisibility' on the initiate responsible for directing the slaughter. The assassin's curse would then be to remain forever present, unseen by those who search for him. Jack is so much there that he merges with the stones, the moss, the grid of future streets.[5]

These words echo Solomon Weil's theory that the Golem is the emanation of London's spiritual sickness. They also bring to mind Ackroyd's theory of the existence of intangible 'patterns of habitation, and patterns of inheritance which seem to emerge from the very streets and alleys of the capital',[6] and help explain why the deaths of Jane Quig, Alice Stanton and Solomon Weil seem to follow the pattern of the Ripper murders even though they were perpetrated ten years in advance: from a mythical perspective, the question of chronology is immaterial, for time is cyclical and human actions are endlessly accumulated and repeated around the same power-concentrating places.

Apart from the ritual murders of the city's scapegoats, the 'whores' and the 'Jew', the Limehouse Golem has also murdered the Guerrard family. This massacre closely follows the pattern established by another Victorian massacre, the John Williams murders – also called the Ratcliffe Highway murders – of 1812, which were raised to the category of 'awful' art by Thomas de

Quincey in his essay *On Murder Considered as One of the Fine Arts.*[7] George Gissing published an article on it, 'Romanticism and Crime' (*DLLG* 112) in which he celebrates de Quincey's ability to transform the bright yellow-haired butcher into a 'wonderful Romantic hero' (*DLLG* 37). Needless to say, the Golem sees its murderous work in this romantic light, and de Quincey's essay is discussed by George Gissing, Dan Leno, Elizabeth Cree, Carl Marx and Chief Inspector Kildare, who have either read, or are on the point of reading it.

The parallelisms between the Guerrard and the Marr families – already suggested by the phonetic closeness of Gue-*rrard* and M-*arr* – are carefully drawn by the very Limehouse Golem: the Guerrards lived in the Marrs' house, they had continued the Marrs' business, the murders were equally committed during the night and carried out with a mallet, and, each time, one female member of the household survived. That is, we can say that the two families were linked by what Ackroyd would call a double 'pattern of habitation' and 'of inheritance'.[8] In this sense, the fact that John Cree's father (another of Elizabeth Cree's victims) should also be a hosier (*DLLG* 256) is also significant, as is the fact that John Cree should have married a music-hall comedian who, like Dan Leno, specialized in crossdressing.

After finding the mutilated body of Alice Stanton wearing a second-hand riding outfit that had belonged to Dan Leno and which she had bought at the Guerrards' (*DLLG* 201), the police become aware of a connection between the murderer and the music-hall comedian, but cannot understand its meaning. Chief Inspector Kildare even associates this murder with the scene in which Dan Leno was nearly strangled on the stage by a killer he took for a male actor. But, a diminished Sherlock Holmes who thinks smoking a pipe will help him 'cogitate' but does not (*DLLG* 257), Kildare does not take up Leno's clue when he tells him that 'It was a she'. The chief inspector was also puzzled by the theatricality of the murders, but he dismisses the impression 'as too fanciful'. By contrast, Dan Leno seems to be aware of the true nature of the massacres, not only because he can identify with the victims through empathy, but because he knows the murderer is a woman who, like himself, is used to crossdressing. Still, he believes that there is nothing to be done but wait: 'the badness will pass in time' (*DLLG* 201–6).

As the reader of Elizabeth Cree's diary eventually learns, this woman is Leno's music-hall partner. The daughter of a reformed prostitute turned Methodist bigot (*DLLG* 12), Elizabeth may be considered as a living emblem of the monsters bred by Utilitarian mercantilism and Methodist repression in the slums of London. The walls of the dingy room where she lived with her mother were literally covered with pages torn from the Bible. In the literal sense, therefore, her eventual metamorphosis into a golem was brought about by the manipulation of holy words: the words that catch her eye after having poisoned her mother refer both to Abraham, the earliest creator of golems, and to Lazarus, who was called back from the dead (*DLLG* 14). From then on, the stages in her transformation from child to monster will invariably follow the murder of a relative or acquaintance.

Peter Keating has noted that, in the novel, 'Dan Leno was born on December 20, 1850, and that, "curiously enough", this was also the birthday of Elizabeth Cree [...]. "In fact", Leno was born exactly ten years later'.[9] The reviewer does not see any reason why Leno's career should be so 'inexplicably compressed'. However, Solomon Weil gives a clue as to the nature of Leno's and Elizabeth's relationship when he explains to Marx that Dan Leno impersonating Sister Anne in *Bluebeard* is not 'the shadow female. It is male and female joined. It is Adam Kadmon, The Universal Man' (*DLLG* 67). From this mythical perspective, Dan Leno, the (historical) male transvestite impersonator of Sister Anne, and Elizabeth Cree, the (fictional) female transvestite impersonator of Bluebeard, may be said to stand in a *Doppelgänger* relationship, with Leno embodying the comic, or 'white' emanation, and Elizabeth Cree the tragic, or 'black' emanation of 'perpetual, infinite London' (*DLLG* 246). This 'self/shadow' complementarity is made explicit by a Hebrew passerby who, almost colliding with Elizabeth Cree dressed as 'The Older Brother', 'just by the Limehouse church [...] muttered something like "Cab man" or "Cadmon"' (*DLLG* 154).[10]

Likewise, this mythical interpretation would give sense to the puzzling fact that some of the murders committed by the Limehouse Golem in 1880 seem to *follow* the pattern established by the Jack the Ripper murders of 1888 even though they antedate them. The Golem murders absorb the John Williams murders and forerun the Ripper murders as they form part of an ever-growing cyclical pattern of horror materializing out of the suffering of the inhabitants of that deprived and degenerate area of Victorian London. Indeed, this interpretation would be compatible both with Marx's contention that 'Murder [...] is the symptom, not the cause, of a great disease', and with Solomon Weil's belief that the world always knows 'what we need, or expect, or dream of, and then it creates such things for us' (*DLLG* 93, 69).

When she was a little child, Elizabeth's mother used to 'pinch it [a place between her legs] fiercely, or prick it with her needle, in order to teach me that it was the home of pain and punishment' (*DLLG* 13). This act of brutal sexual repression is at the core of Elizabeth's transformation into the Limehouse Golem and explains both her utter frigidity and the ritual mutilations she inflicted on some of her victims. Although she married John Cree, she never allowed him to have sexual intercourse with her. And after the timely death of his father of 'gastric fever' (in fact, Elizabeth's poisoning of him) 'just at the time we were visiting him in Lancashire' (*DLLG* 256), she hired as maid (and, as she hoped, as her husband's mistress too) a young actress called Aveline Mortimer, whom she hated because she had played a dirty trick on her in the old times and also because she was, like herself, an illegitimate child. When Aveline gets pregnant, Elizabeth destroys the unborn infant (*DLLG* 256), and then starts poisoning her husband, who already suspects her of being the Golem. This is her last crime for, thanks to Aveline's testimony, she is imprisoned, tried and sentenced to death for his murder.

After inheriting his father's fortune, John Cree had given up the job of newspaper reporter in order to write a social drama about the condition of the London poor, entitled *Misery Junction*. However, Elizabeth, who was hoping to impersonate the central character, is incapable of waiting for her husband to finish it and hurriedly writes her own version, unwittingly transforming 'Catherine Dove, the poor orphan girl' into a parody of her own 'dark life' (*DLLG* 231–2) in which her evil nature is given away. Unable to sell the play, she hires the theatre for one night and fills it with 'all the loiterers and dawdlers of Limehouse'. As happened before with her music-hall impersonations, Elizabeth sees her new role as 'a new life for me upon the stage'. Therefore, when her interpretation is met with the 'general laughter' of the riotous crowd, she gives up attempting to deny her origins and to escape her fate. Seeing 'her own anxiety and bewilderment' reflected in 'the faces of the fallen women all lit up by the gas, grinning and yawning', she mildly accepts her last role: that of scapegoat of the social degeneracy of Limehouse (*DLLG* 236–42). Elizabeth's last transformation to scapegoat comes full circle when, like the prostitutes she had ritually mutilated, she endures the ritual (forensic) mutilation of her head and brains (*DLLG* 2, 274) at the hands of the London authorities.

The novel ends with the performance of the 'authoritative version of *Misery Junction*' (*DLLG* 276), which, ironically enough, is an 'improved' version of Elizabeth's version of John Cree's play. The heroine's name (Catherine Dove) was changed to 'Elizabeth Cree' and her part was to be played by Aveline Mortimer. The play begins exactly like *Dan Leno and the Limehouse Golem*, 'with the execution of Elizabeth Cree in the yard of Camberwell Prison'. The audience is awe-stricken and delighted. But Leno realizes that 'something had gone terribly wrong [...] and that the neck of Aveline Mortimer must surely be broken as she dangled beneath the stage'. And it is Dan Leno who, as he had so often done before, improvised a solution: 'clambering up the fatal rope in the dress of Madame Gruyère', he revived Elizabeth Cree in another guise 'just as she had been before when she played the "Older Brother" or "Little Victor's Daughter", and it was a source of joy and exhilaration that the great Dan Leno should impersonate her' (*DLLG* 276–82).

Thus Dan Leno, the music-hall monopolylinguist, puts an end to the cycle of evil absorbing the Limehouse Golem and transforms it into a humorous and harmless music-hall transvestite character. With it, the chaotic phase comes to an end, order is restored and life in London can begin a new cycle, for the city that has bred the Golem is also the city that has bred the comedian/magus capable of absorbing it and expelling it in the cathartic ritual of drama. Indeed, Leno's rare art of impersonation is comparable to the drug-induced trances of the Sphinx at Delphi, or of tribal 'medicine men': 'He drank wildly and incessantly until he woke the following morning without a care in the world. He knew that, in his drunkenness, he would enact many of his familiar characters [...]. When he woke up [...] he felt much at peace, as if he had performed an exorcism' (*DLLG* 204).

De Quincey explains that the corpse of John Williams had been buried 'in the centre of a quadrivium, [...] with a stake driven through his heart' (*DLLG* 275). More rationalist, though equally ineffective, were the measures taken in the case of Elizabeth Cree: her head was severed, her brain analysed for malformations, and her body 'covered with quicklime to encourage speedy decomposition' (*DLLG* 274). We know that, for all these precautions, the Golem will be attracted again to the same 'evil quarter mile' of London in 1888, as Jack the Ripper, when the old wisdom preserved in the popular songs and ballads will again be forgotten and Londoners will once more allow the material world to take the form of 'The World Without Love'.

In September 1996, Ackroyd published his latest novel to date, *Milton in America*. With it, the writer puts an end to the series of London-based novels and takes us on a journey with John Milton (1608–74) to the New World. The novel fictionalizes the possibility that, instead of staying in England in order to publish *Paradise Lost* (1667) and *Paradise Regained* (1671), Milton would have fled England after the downfall of the Commonwealth during the few months preceding the arrival of Charles II at the beginning of 1660, in order to build a Puritan paradise in the New World. It thus situates itself within the tradition of the American historical romance that goes back to Charles Brockden Brown's *Wieland* (1798), 'the first of many American tales to record the story of the new American Eden and the fall that took place there'.[11]

Milton sees himself from the start as a mythological hero with the colossal task of creating the perfect Commonwealth in New England, a task comparable to the work of the Creation in six days which, according to *Paradise Lost*, God accomplished through the agency of his Son.[12] After the shipwreck, Milton and Goosequill, his amanuensis and guide, come upon the summit of a hill and the boy sees ahead of him 'valleys and hills, woods and lakes, and white mountains in the far distance' spreading in perfect harmony reminiscent of the 'order in variety' of Pope's 'Windsor Forest'. On hearing this description, Milton enthusiastically concludes that 'We have come out of Sodom into the land of Canaan', but as soon as he utters these words, he loses his balance and slips over the edge of a cliff (*MA* 69). His fall is in fact stopped by a providential tree, but although there is an Edenic spring that eventually grows into a stream, the stream runs along the edge of a great threatening forest and leads to a clearing where 'the ground was scorched and blackened'. And Milton's paradisal dream 'that we were in a great forest [with] many turtle-doves [...] cooing' is interrupted when 'the flies woke me'. Indeed, the only edible fruit they find is a sweet 'dark berry [hanging] in many luscious clusters' that unexpectedly dissolves 'into a cloud of wasps' (*MA* 71, 73, 76).

The archetypal good/evil nature of the New World is enhanced by Milton's remark at the beginning of the novel that New England looks like 'a sleeper ready to awake' (*MA* 10). This image brings to mind Doctor Dee's hieroglyphic monad, and also Blake's Albion, a figure which represents England and the prelapsarian and universal human form of all being, and which Blake describes in *Milton, a Poem* as either dead,[13] or asleep.[14] In other words, the image suggests that New England is a whole Self/World in need of (spiritual) awakening. When he started the journey, Milton was convinced that his task was precisely that of awakening this sleeper to the 'true' faith. However, after being lost in the wilderness for two days, like Christ when he was tempted by the Devil in the desert, he begins to wonder whether God has sent him to New England in order to raise 'Eden in this wilderness' or whether the journey was 'a divine punishment' (*MA* 74). This terrible doubt is going to torment Milton throughout the novel and to determine his future behaviour.

When the Puritan settlers ask Milton to lead them in the construction and government of their new settlement, Milton submits his leadership to a general vote and insists that 'Where men are equal they ought to have an equal interest in government' (*MA* 111). However, Milton's plan for the construction of New Milton is based on a Manichean separation of the 'elect' from the 'evil', evident from the Puritans' self-imposed title: 'Particular Separatist Elect' (*MA* 144).[15] And the settlement is ruled according to strict repressive laws, justified by Milton's conviction that virtue is unattainable without religion and the dictates of moral law.

By contrast, Mary Mount, the nearby Catholic and Indian settlement, is based on a kind of egalitarianism that brings to mind the religious toleration reigning in Thomas More's *Utopia*. The colourful and disorderly display of the people's garments and rites is also reminiscent of the 'multi-coloured vestments' of the Utopian priests, 'decorated with the feathers of various birds'.[16] These colours and feathers may be said to symbolize prelapsarian bliss, and contrast with the black garments and sickly pallid faces of the brethren following Milton's repressive rules, which seem exclusively aimed at destroying all sources of happiness, from pastimes such as drinking, music or dancing, to the laughter of children (*MA* 193, 163), which, according to T. S. Eliot, symbolizes the innocent pleasure of Eden before the Fall.[17]

Indeed, the most characteristic trait of the Mary Mount settlers is their preternatural merriment, which (besides the phonetic similarity of the names of both settlements) aligns them to the carnivalesque world of Nathaniel Hawthorne's sketch 'The Maypole of Merry Mount'.[18] In this sketch, a 'New England annalist' records the history of the 'gay colony' of Mount Wollaston or Merry Mount, the site of an early trading company near Plymouth, Massachusetts, presided over by that ancestral emblem of seasonal renewal, the maypole. The narrator–annalist explains how in those days 'Jollity and gloom were contending for an empire' and how, 'should their banner be triumphant, [the settlers of Merry Mount] were to pour sunshine over New England's rugged hills, and scatter flower seeds throughout the soil'.[19]

It is easy to see the parallelism between 'the grim Puritans'[20] in Hawthorne's tale and the 'Particular Separatist Elect' in New Milton, and between the 'mirthful spirit dwell[ing] all the year round at Merry Mount[21] and the jollity of Indians and Catholics at Mary Mount, but the narrow-mindedness of Milton and his Particular Separatist Elect also brings to mind William Blake's criticism of the Puritan writer. In *Milton, a Poem*, the visionary poet and engraver offers the author of *Paradise Lost* the possibility of returning from heaven to the earth in order to mend the errors committed in his earlier life. As Essick and Viscomi have pointed out, 'In Blake's view, Milton's errors infected his life and writings with classical paganism, moral self-righteousness, and rational materialism'.[22] Blake condemns Milton's use of the 'single vision' of rational materialism (what he called 'Newton's sleep') as utterly reductionist and evil.

On 20 December 1661 Milton, who has gone out for a walk into the forest, falls into an Indian deer trap and finds himself 'hanging from a pole [suspended] between earth and heaven [. . .]. His dark world turned upside down' (*MA* 158). He then discovers in amazement that he can see (*MA* 159). That is, Milton finds himself in the position of the Hanged Man, the Tarot card symbolizing the quester's opportunity to destroy 'the whole "higher" structure of outlook, attitudes, tastes, acquired mental and emotional habits, which cages the inner man'.[23] Rescued by the friendly Powpows, Milton experiences the soothing and healing power of the *sachem*'s sympathetic magic. In other words, he is given the opportunity to correct his 'single vision' with the magical and mythical knowledge of the Indians. However, he stubbornly refuses to accept magic as good and concludes that these 'rare cures in the wilderness must surely be the work of the devil' (*MA* 216–17).

Analysing the figure of Satan in *Paradise Lost*, C. S. Lewis has noted that 'Satan in his speech shows complete inability to conceive any state of mind but the infernal'.[24] Milton's incapacity to think otherwise than infernally reaches its climax during the Indian 'feast of dreams', when he mistakes the pure prelapsarian 'mix[ture of] soul with soul, or flesh with flesh', offered him by the Indian virgin, for guilty sex, 'the cause of all his woe' (*MA* 275). The rejection of this opportunity to grow spiritually brings about the return of Milton's (spiritual and physical) blindness and confirms his self-fragmentation into (to adapt Blake's words) a 'sleep-walking body' and (a condemned) 'immortal Self',[25] expressed in Milton's narrative voice split into the first and the third person. At this stage, he reaches the point of no return when the quester, incapable of being reborn into a new spiritual life, becomes a 'Black Brother isolated from the rest of the universe in the hard and evil shell of his own egotism'. Deprived of spiritual nourishment, 'Such a being is gradually disintegrated [. . .]. He may indeed prosper for a while, but in the end he must perish'.[26]

It is after his return from the Indian camp that Milton

promulgates the most drastically punitive and repressive laws and undertakes a tour of the main Puritan towns in New England in order to 'raise an army of the Lord utterly to destroy [the] papists' of Mary Mount (MA 242). The battle for the recovery of Heaven in Paradise Lost (Book VI) ends with the glorious victory of the Messiah. By contrast, in this battle, Mary Mount is destroyed, and Ralph Kempis and Goosequill die, together with most of the Catholics, while the Indians are unmercifully massacred. Thus, the novel seems to end with Milton's imposition of Doctor Dee's nightmarish 'World Without Love'. However, we could say that the death of Kempis/ Michael foreruns the sacrifice of Christ, while the death of Milton's pupil would be in keeping with the akedah, the sacrifice of Isaac by his father Abraham, a recurrent topos in the American historical romance which, according to Emily Miller Budick,

> defined and guaranteed the essential movement of American history, from its exodus from England through its entry into Canaan to its establishment of a Puritan theocracy in the New World. The moment of the akedah, then, is the point at which Old Testament, New Testament, and American history begins and begins anew – or ought to begin.[27]

Vieland and the other Abraham figures in the American historical romances expected to establish a Puritan theocracy through the sacrifice of their sons, but achieved instead personal and communal disaster. Likewise, Milton's victory over Goosequill and Kempis is Pyrrhic, for, as the angels point out in Paradise Lost, whoever tries to rebel against God brings about a result that is the opposite of what s/he intended (Book VII, line 613). And it should not be forgotten that, at the end of the novel, Milton's fragmented Self is left sadly narrating how his own sleep-walking Shadow, condemned like Adam (but without Eve), 'wandered ahead and, weeping, through the dark wood took his solitary way' (MA 277).

Milton's condemnation to wander in solitude is an adequate punishment for his sin of individualism. As a Puritan, he believed in the unique significance of the individual calling towards God and in the doctrine of justification by faith alone. These beliefs justified his refusal to listen to others or to take into consideration beliefs and ideas differing from his own. But it should not be forgotten that, from a Catholic perspective, these cornerstones of Protestantism were heresies that had caused Martin Luther to be excommunicated.

Ackroyd has often explained that he usually works on two different manuscripts at the same time, writing one book in the morning and researching for another in the afternoon. After the publication of *Blake* (1995), Ackroyd continued working on *Milton in America*, Ackroyd continued working on *Milton in America* (1996) and started collecting material for *The Life of Thomas More* (1998), his latest biography to date. We noted above the influence of Blake's *Milton, A Poem* (and we would also add Blake's poem *America*) on *Milton in America*, and how the colourful display of the Mary Mount settlers echoes the religious toleration and prelapsarian bliss reigning in Thomas More's *Utopia*. Certainly, there are many other details in the novel which Ackroyd owes to Thomas More. For example, before the shipwreck of the *Gabriel*, Goosequill describes the white cliffs of the Massachusetts coast to Milton, saying that they are arranged 'in the shape of a half-moon, with two arms outstretched towards us'. The comparison with a half-moon brings to mind Raphael Hythlodaeus's description of the island of Utopia 'as a sort of crescent'.[28] However, Milton immediately associates these white cliffs with 'those of Dover' (12), an association made more significant by Ackroyd's remark in *The Life of Thomas More* that the dimensions of Utopia 'are the same as those of England and the number of its city-states are the same number of English counties together with London [...]. Its principal city, Amaurotum, is [...] London redrawn by visionary imagination, a pristine city in which [...] there is no greed or pride or disorder' (*LTM* 167). In other words, Goosequill's and Milton's apparently banal remarks – like Milton's description of New England as 'a sleeper ready to awake' – enhance the condition of New England as a 'self/world' or 'mystical city', in the Catholic tradition that runs from St Augustine's *City of God* to William Blake's Albion:

> In Augustine's work the history of the world is conceived in terms of these two cities, the city of the world and the city of God, distinct but not entirely separate, together experiencing 'the vicissitudes of time'. The heavenly city exists within the earthly city, in separate individuals or in communities of believers, so that it is possible to see

within the fallen city – let us say, London – 'an image of the Heavenly City [...]. The city of the world could aspire, at least, to the condition of the city of God. (*LTM* 102).

In the biography, Ackroyd underlines as one of the most important sources of disagreement between Catholics and Lutherans at the time of the Reformation the question of whether the true state is a congregation of believers ruled by the intervention of grace and divine law, or an association of men ruled by national law and positive law (*LTM* 102). Thomas More 'believed himself to be part of a larger spiritual community (the living and the dead together)', and he considered 'this world as a stage in which each must play a part' (*LTM* 102, 103). Ackroyd points out how, for late fifteenth- and early sixteenth-century Catholics, the body of Christ 'was considered not only to be the transubstantiated host, but also the entire Catholic Church from its beginning in human history', and how there are intimations in More's writings 'of Christian society making up one physical body'. Ackroyd interprets this, in words that bring to mind Doctor Dee's and Blake's mystical visions of London, as 'a symbolic and imaginative order in which Christ, the eucharist and the Church partake of the flesh and the blood and are incarnated in the heart of the city' (*LTM* 110, 111).

This mystical interpretation of Christian society as the physical body of Christ involved a strong sense of the sacredness of place, expressed, for example, in the proliferation of processions and other elaborate rituals organised on occasion of the numerous festivals and holy days of the ritual year. One of the most popular was precisely that of the 'May Day'. As Ackroyd explains, London had then 'many Maypoles, with a "knape" or bunch of flowers on its top, so high that it towered over the steeple of the church itself' (*LTM* 112). The narrator in Nathaniel Hawthorne's 'The Maypole of Merry Mount' constantly associates the lively rituals of this festival with those of classical paganism. He calls them 'people of the Golden Age' and compares them to 'Fauns and Nymphs',[29] while the Puritans in *Milton in America* are scandalized by the assimilation of Indian and Catholic rites in Mary Mount. Similarly, in the biography, Ackroyd notes that: 'On May Day itself the king and queen rode out from Greenwich Palace, and on their way were met by "Robin Hood" with two hundred archers dressed in green garments; the royal pair were invited to dine in a wood near Shooters Hill' (*LTM* 160). The plasticity of the description, with the unexpectedly large number of archers dressed in green, succinctly conveys the pagan spirit of seasonal renewal characteristic of May Day, whose living emblem is the 'Green Man'. This festive spirit and the unmitigated love of ritual and ceremony found many other forms of expression in the numerous liturgical ceremonies of Thomas More's Catholic England (*LTM* 112). All of them convey the spirit of the medieval Catholic European visionary culture Ackroyd – and Hawthorne's narrator – yearns for, and which the Puritans strove to eradicate.

For a Catholic like Thomas More the Church was not a simple aggregate of believers, in the same way the Catholic Europe he worked all his life to pacify and unify, was not a simple aggregate of nations, or the law he practised just a set of utilitarian rules. The Church was nothing less than 'the mystical body of Christ, comprising the living and the dead [...] the vehicle of God's purpose and the paradigm of all earthly law and authority (*LTM* 275), in the same way Catholic Europe was the physical body of Christ, and human law the reflection of divine Law. From More's perspective, therefore, the Protestants' attempts to deny the authority of the Church and to interpret the inherited dogmas individually could only be interpreted as evidence of the coming of the Antichrist and the approach of Doomsday itself.

Ackroyd makes an important point when he notes that the basic difference between Post-Reformation and Catholic culture lies in what he describes as 'the great moments of Protestant affirmation', expressed, for example, in Luther's words: 'Here I stand. Here I remain. Here I glory. Here I triumph' (*LTM* 225). From Luther's exultant affirmation of selfhood to the Cartesian *cogito* and the materialistic 'single vision' Blake called 'Newton's sleep', there are only two further logical steps in the same direction. In other words, More's faith was a medieval faith based on order and ritual, where the anonymous conscience was led by the unchallenged historical authority of the church, while Luther's faith was that of the Renaissance Christian, a faith fully possessed of the authentic voice of the free, individual conscience of Man. This is the crucial ideological divide that gives Sir Thomas More's death historical sense.

The Life of Thomas More occupies an indispensable place in the constellation of Peter Ackroyd's writings. In this new, bestselling biography, Ackroyd mixes straight narrative and anecdotes borrowed from More's earlier biographies with fragments taken from extant records and also lost letters, dialogues, depositions, Parliamentary sessions and set-piece medieval liturgies, such a penitential prayers or the wonderful description of Thomas More's baptism with which the biography starts, thus creating a characteristic Ackroydian 'landscape of the imagination'[30] midway between history, biography and literature that forcefully impels the reader to imagine the busy and colourful London of Thomas More's days and to recreate the life of an exceptional witness to the last years of Catholicism and the advent of Anglicanism in England.

Needless to say, this historical period is crucial for Ackroyd, as it heralds the decline of that highly mysterious and magical religion with ancestral pagan roots Ackroyd acknowledges as his own, and whose traces inform the work of 'monopolylinguists' like Charles Mathews and Dan Leno, and of 'Cockney visionary writers' like Oscar Wilde, Chatterton, Dickens, Blake, Iain Sinclair or Peter Ackroyd himself, writers, that is, who have a strong sense of the sacredness of place and of communal bondage, and try to exorcise the fear of darkness through the visionary potential of art and literature.

Notes

CHAPTER 1. ONLY CONNECT...

1. In Susana Onega, 'An Interview with Peter Ackroyd', *Twentieth-Century Literature*, vol. 42, no. 2. (summer 1996), 209.
2. John Walsh, 'Confessions of a Monopolylinguist', *Sunday Times*, 17 May 1992, section 6, p. 4.
3. *The Curiously Strong*, vol. iii, no. 6 (24 March 1971).
4. Onega, 'An Interview with Peter Ackroyd', 210–11.
5. *Partisan Review*, vol. xliv, no. 2 (1977) 262–3.
6. Peter Conrad, '*Notes for a New Culture*: An Essay on Modernism', *Times Literary Supplement (TLS)*, 3 December 1976, 1524.
7. Ibid.
8. Ibid.
9. David Lodge, 'Mine, Of Course', *New Statesman*, 19 March 1976, p. 364.
10. Onega, 'An Interview with Peter Ackroyd', 210.
11. Blake Morrison, *The Movement: English Poetry and Fiction of the 1950s* (London: Oxford University Press, 1980).
12. Grevel Lindop, 'The Empty Telephone Boys', *PN Review*, vol. 15, no. 6 (1989), 44.
13. In A. Norman Jeffares (ed.), *Poems of W. B. Yeats* (1962; London: Macmillan, 1985), 121.
14. In Walford Dawes (ed.), *William Wordsworth: Selected Poems* (London: Everyman's University Library, 1975), 39.
15. T. S. Eliot, *Collected Poems (1909–1962)* (London: Faber & Faber, 1974), 89–90.
16. In Ian Hamilton (ed.), *The Oxford Companion to Twentieth-Century Poetry* (Oxford and New York: Oxford University Press, 1994), 119.
17. In Ian Gregson, 'Epigraphs and Epigones: John Ashbery's Influence in England', *Bête Noire*, 4 (winter 1987), 89.
18. Edward Larrissy, *Reading Twentieth-Century Poetry: The Language of Gender and Objects* (Oxford: Basil Blackwell, 1990), 183.
19. Introduction to *The Penguin Book of Contemporary British Poetry*

(Harmondsworth: Penguin, 1982), 15.

20. Eliot, *Collected Poems*, 65.
21. Ibid., 216.
22. Ibid., 63.
23. Ibid.
24. Ibid., 71.
25. Ibid, 74.
26. In *The Oxford Book of Twentieth-Century English Verse*, chosen by Philip Larkin (Oxford and New York: Oxford University Press, 1988), 447.
27. Linda Hutcheon, *A Poetics of Postmodernism: History, Theory, Fiction* (New York and London: Routledge, 1988), 5.
28. Eliot, *Collected Poems*, 64–5.
29. Richard Cavendish, *The Magical Arts: Western Occultism and Occultists* (London: Arkana, 1984), 81–3.

CHAPTER 2. LORD OF LANGUAGE AND LORD OF LIFE

1. Patrick McGrath, 'Peter Ackroyd', *Bomb*, 26 (winter 1988–9), 44–7.
2. Onega, 'An Interview with Peter Ackroyd', 210.
3. Ibid., 212.
4. Steve Ellis, '*Ezra Pound and His World*', *TLS*, 28 August 1981, p. 989.
5. Francis King, 'Lusty Début', *Spectator*, 30 January 1982, p. 20.
6. Mary Montaut, '*The Last Testament of Oscar Wilde*', *Irish University Review*, vol. 14, no. 1 (1984), 136–9.
7. Ibid.
8. Peter Ackroyd, 'London Luminaries and Cockney Visionaries', *The LWT London Lecture* (Victoria and Albert Museum, 7 December 1993).
9. See, for example, Michael Neve's 'The Living Dead', *History Today*, 38 (January 1988), 53–4.
10. Michael Worton and Juliet Still, Introduction to *Intertextuality: Theories and Practices* (Manchester and New York: Manchester University Press, 1990), 13.
11. Peter Ackroyd, *Blake* (London: Sinclair-Stevenson, 1995), 351.
12. Ibid., 367.

CHAPTER 3. A DREAM OF WHOLENESS AND OF BEAUTY

1. Iain Sinclair, *Lud Heat: A Book of the Dead Hamlets* (London: Albion Village Press, 1975).
2. Ibid., 5.
3. Ibid., 10.
4. Ibid.

5. Ibid., 5.
6. On this, see Onega, 'Pattern and Magic in *Hawksmoor*', *Atlantis*, vol. xii, no. 2 (November 1991), 34.
7. On the differences between the *Scientia Umbrarum* and the New Science, see Onega, 'Empiricism and the "Scientia Umbrarum" in *Hawksmoor*', in Francisco Collado (ed.), *Science, Literature and Interpretation: Essays on Twentieth-Century Literature and Critical Theory* (Zaragoza: Servicio de Publicaciones de la Universidad de Zaragoza, 1991), 117–38.
8. Richard Cavendish, *The Magical Arts: Western Occultism and Occultists* (London: Arkana, 1984), 13, 17.
9. Claude Rawson, 'Peter Ackroyd: *First Light*', *TLS*, 28 April–4 May 1989, p. 453.
10. Ioannis Dee, *Monas Hieroglyphica* (Antverpiae, 1564), theorem vi, p. 12.
11. In Peter Ackroyd, *Blake* (London: Sinclair-Stevenson, 1995), 58.
12. T. S. Eliot, *Collected Poems (1909–1962)* (London: Faber & Faber, 1974), 89–90.
13. Prospero has been thought to reflect John Dee. See, Frances A. Yates, *Giordano Bruno and the Hermetic Tradition* (London: Routledge and Kegan Paul and Chicago: The University of Chicago Press, 1977), 357.

CHAPTER 4. THE BADNESS WILL PASS IN TIME

1. Peter Keating, 'Here We Are Again!', *Times Literary Supplement*, 9 September 1994, p. 21.
2. Peter Ackroyd, 'London Luminaries and Cockney Visionaries'.
3. Peter Ackroyd, *The House of Doctor Dee* (London: Hamish Hamilton, 1993), 266.
4. E. W. Chick, 'A Question of Identity and Motive', in Camila Wolff (compiler), *Who Was Jack the Ripper? A Collection of Present-Day Theories and Observations* (London: Greyhound Books, 1995), 21.
5. Iain Sinclair, 'Unnaming the Nameless', in Camila Wolff (compiler), *Who Was Jack the Ripper?*, 73.
6. Peter Ackroyd, 'London Luminaries and Cockney Visionaries'.
7. Thomas de Quincey, *On Murder Considered as One of the Fine Arts* (London: Holerth Press, 1926).
8. Ackroyd, 'London Luminaries and Cockney Visionaries'.
9. Keating, 'Here We Are Again!', 21.
10. The reversibility and complementarity of Dan Leno and Elizabeth Cree is also, incidentally, revealed by the fact that the American edition of the novel is entitled *The Trial of Elizabeth Cree*.

11. Emily Miller Budick, *Fiction and Historical Consciousness: The American Romance Tradition* (New Haven and London: Yale University Press, 1989), 26.
12. 'and thou my Word, begotten Son, by thee/ This I perform, speak thou, and be it done' (*Paradise Lost*, Book VII, lines 162–3).
13. In Robert N. Essick and Joseph Viscomi (eds.), *William Blake: Milton, a Poem and the Final Illuminated Works* (London: The William Blake Trust/The Tate Gallery, 1993), plate 2(b), line 1.
14. Ibid., plate 22, lines 3–5.
15. Their name parodies that of the 'Separatists', the more radical Puritan faction. Before the Civil Wars, many 'Separatists' went into exile in America, thus becoming the 'Pilgrims' who settled in Plymouth, Massachusetts, in the 1620s. Many more joined them after the collapse of the Commonwealth.
16. Thomas More, *Utopia*, translated with an introduction by Paul Turner (Harmondsworth: Penguin, 1971), 127.
17. 'the leaves were full of children,/ Hidden excitedly, containing laughter' (T. S. Eliot, *Collected Poems (1909–1962)*, 190).
18. Nathaniel Hawthorne, 'The Maypole of Merry Mount', in Thomas E. Connolly (ed.), *Nathaniel Hawthorne, 'The Scarlet Letter' and Selected Tales* (Harmondsworth: Penguin, 1978), 287–98.
19. Ibid., 287.
20. Ibid., 293.
21. Ibid., 287.
22. Robert N. Essick and Joseph Viscomi (eds.), Introduction to *William Blake: Milton, a Poem*.
23. Cavendish, *The Magical Arts*, 108–9.
24. C. S. Lewis, *A Preface to 'Paradise Lost'* (London: Oxford University Press, 1975).
25. In Robert N. Essick and Joseph Viscomi (eds.), *William Blake: Milton, a Poem*, plate 14, lines 1–7.
26. Cavendish, *The Magical Arts*, 111.
27. Budick, *Fiction and Historical Consciousness*, 37.
28. More, *Utopia*, 69.
29. Hawthorne, 'The Maypole of Merry Mount', 288.
30. Peter Stanford, 'Church of Past Times', *Independent on Sunday*, 1 March 1998, 26.

Select Bibliography

WORKS BY PETER ACKROYD

Poetry
All poetry references are to first publication in volume form.

Ouch (London: The Curiously Strong Press, 1971).
London Lickpenny (London: Ferry Press, 1973).
Country Life (London: Ferry Press, 1978).
The Diversions of Purley and Other Poems (London: Abacus, 1987).
'Three Poems by Peter Ackroyd', in John Ashbery (ed.), 'New English Poets', *Partisan Review*, vol. xliv, no. 2 (1977), 245–67.

Critical Essays
Notes for a New Culture (1976; repr. London: Alkin Books, 1993).
Dressing Up: Transvestism and Drag, the History of an Obsession (London: Thames & Hudson, 1979).

Biographies
Ezra Pound and his World (London: Thames & Hudson, 1980). Printed in the United States as *Ezra Pound*.
T. S. Eliot (London: Cardinal, 1984). Printed in the United States as *T. S. Eliot, A Life*.
Dickens (London: Sinclair-Stevenson, 1990). Printed in the United States as *Dickens, Life and Times*.
Introduction to Dickens (London: Sinclair-Stevenson, 1991).
Blake (London: Sinclair-Stevenson, 1995).
The Life of Thomas More (London: Chatto and Windus, 1998).

Novels
Where possible, reference to the fiction is to first publications.

The Great Fire of London (London: Hamish Hamilton, 1982).
The Last Testament of Oscar Wilde (London: Hamish Hamilton, 1983).
Hawksmoor (London: Hamish Hamilton, 1985).

Chatterton (London: Hamish Hamilton, 1987).
First Light (London: Hamish Hamilton, 1989).
English Music (London: Hamish Hamilton, 1992).
The House of Doctor Dee (London: Hamish Hamilton, 1993).
Dan Leno and the Limehouse Golem (London: Sinclair-Stevenson, 1994). Printed in the United States as *The Trial of Elizabeth Cree.*
Milton in America (London: Sinclair-Stevenson, 1996).

Lectures

'London Luminaries and Cockney Visionaries', *The LWT London Lecture* (Victoria and Albert Museum, 7 December 1993). Edited extract from lecture printed as 'Cockney Visionaries', *Independent*, 18 December 1993, p. 27.
'Blake and London Radicalism', *The TLS Talk* (Royal Festival Hall, 28 October 1995)
'The Englishness of English Literature', *XIX AEDEAN Conference* (Vigo, 16 December 1995). In *Proceedings of the XIXth International Conference of AEDEAN*, ed. Javier Pérez Guerra, (Departamento de Filoloxía Inglesa e Alemana, Universidade de Vigo, 1996), 11–19.

Short Stories

'The Plantation House', *New Statesman and Society Christmas Supplement* 1991, 26–32.

Critical Editions and Introductions

PEN New Fiction I, edited by Peter Ackroyd (London, Melbourne and New York: Quartet Books, 1984).
Dickens' London: An Imaginative Vision, introduced by Peter Ackroyd, text by Piers Dudgen (1987), (London: Headline, 1994), 7–20.
Oscar Wilde: The Picture of Dorian Gray, edited by Peter Ackroyd (London: Penguin, 1985).
Poems of William Blake, selected and introduced by Peter Ackroyd (London: Sinclair-Stevenson, 1995).

Uncollected Essays

'Oscar Wilde: Comedy as Tragedy', *New York Times Book Review*, 1 November 1987, p. 14.
'Classic Selection: Peter Ackroyd makes a personal choice of favourite books', *The Good Book Guide*, 65 (November–December 1993), 18.
'Autobiography of a House', *House and Garden*, vol. 164, no. 5 (May 1992), 36, 40, 42.
'My Interpretation of Dreams: A Time Machine', *The Times*, 21 August 1996.

INTERVIEWS WITH PETER ACKROYD

Appleyard, Brian, 'Aspects of Ackroyd', *Sunday Times Magazine*, 9 April 1989, pp. 50–4.

Billen, Andrew, 'Printed Melancholy, Unpublished Giggles', *Observer*, 15 May 1992, p. 60.

Mackenzie, Susie, 'Portrait of an Artist Behaving Badly...', *Arena*, 7 September 1994, p. 12.

McGrath, Patrick, 'Peter Ackroyd', *Bomb*, xxvi (winter 1988–9), 44–7.

Onega, Susana, 'An Interview with Peter Ackroyd', *Twentieth Century Literature*, vol. 42, no. 2 (summer 1996), 208–20.

CRITICAL AND BIOGRAPHICAL STUDIES

General

Herman, Luc, 'Peter Ackroyd', *Post-war Literatures in English*, 7 (March 1990), 9 pp.

Kaveney, Roz, 'Sinclair, Ackroyd and the London Novel', *New Statesman and Society*, 9 September 1994, p. 39.

Kendrick, Walter, 'Peter Ackroyd's Tales from the Crypt', *Village Voice Literary Supplement*, vol. 78, no. v (September 1989), 23–4.

Levis, Peter, 'Fiction at the Centre and on the Fringe', *Stand Magazine*, vol. 30, no. 3 (1989), 66–73.

Miller, Karl, 'Long Live Pastiche', in *Authors* (Oxford: Clarendon Press, 1989), 85–95.

Onega, Susana, 'British Historiographic Metafiction in the 1980s', in *British Postmodern Fiction*, Theo D'haen and Hans Bertens (eds.), Postmodern Studies 7 (Amsterdam and Atlanta: Rodopi, 1993), 47–61.

—— 'British Historiographic Metafiction', in *Metafiction*, Mark Currie (ed.), Longman Critical Readers (London and New York: Longman 1995), 92–103.

—— 'Self, Text and World in British Historiographic Metafiction', *Anglistik. Mitteilungen des Verbandes Deutscher Anglisten*, vol. 2, no. 6 (September 1995), 93–105.

—— 'Palimpsestos transcendentes: las metaficciones historiográficas de Peter Ackroyd', *La Página*, vol. 2, no. 16 (1995), 43–57.

Peck, John, 'The Novels of Peter Ackroyd', *English Studies*, vol. 75, no. 5 (1994), 442–52.

Taylor, D. J., *After the War: The Novel and England since 1945* (London: Chatto and Windus, 1993).

On the Critical Essays
Notes for a New Culture
Conrad, Peter, 'Notes for a New Culture: An Essay on Modernism', TLS (Times Literary Supplement) 3 December 1976, p. 1524.
Lodge, David, 'Mine, Of Course', New Statesman, 19 March 1976, pp. 364–5.

Dressing Up: Transvestism and Drag, the History of an Obsession
Ewart, Gavin, 'Peter Ackroyd: Dressing Up: Transvestism and Drag: the History of an Obsession', TLS, 7 December 1979, p. 96.
Levy, Paul, 'Borrowed Bras', Observer, 16 December 1979, p. 39.

On the Biographies
Ezra Pound and his World
Ellis, Steve, Ezra Pound and His World, TLS, 28 August 1981, p. 989.
Kirstein, Lincoln, 'Ezra Pound and His World', New York Review of Books, 28 (30 April 1981), 3, 6.

T. S. Eliot
Dinnage, Rosemary, 'The Ideal Husband', New York Review of Books, 20 December 1984, pp. 31–2, 34.
Haffenden, John, 'What the Life Leaves Out', TLS, 23 February 1996, pp. 14–15.
Ricks, Christopher, 'The Braver Thing', London Review of Books, 1–14 November 1984, pp. 3–5.
Updike, John, 'Eliot Without Words', New Yorker, 25 March 1985, pp. 120–30.

On the Poetry
Ford, Mark, 'The Diversions of Purley', TLS, 20–26 November 1987, p. 1276.
Gregson, Ian, 'Epigraphs and Epigonees: John Ashbery's Influence in England', Bête Noire, vol. v, no. 4 (winter 1987), 89–94.
Jenkins, Alan, 'The Diversions of Purley', Observer, 22 March 1987, p. 27.
Lindop, Grevel, 'The Empty Telephone Boys', PN Review, vol. 15, no. 6 (1989), 43–6.
McClatchy, J. D., 'Masks and Passions', Poetry, 154 (1989), 29–48.
Porter, Peter, 'Hearts and Sleeves', Observer, 27 January 1974, p. 30.
—— 'Signs of Greatness', Observer, 19 November 1978, p. 39.
Prynne, J. H., 'London Lickpenny', Spectator, 19 January 1974, p. 78.

On the Novels

The Great Fire of London

King, Francis, 'Lusty Début', *Spectator*, 30 January 1982, p. 20.

Strawson, Galen, 'Peter Ackroyd: *The Great Fire of London*', *TLS*, 29 January 1982, p. 105.

Sutherland, John, 'Generations', *London Review of Books*, 4–17 March 1982, pp. 19–20.

The Last Testament of Oscar Wilde

Longford, Frank, 'Oscar', *Spectator*, 16 April 1983, p. 26.

Montaut, Mary, '*The Last Testament of Oscar Wilde*', *Irish University Review*, vol. 14, no. 1 (1984), 136–9.

Paulin, Tom, 'Oscar and Constance', *London Review of Books*, 17–30 November 1983, pp. 20–2.

Hawksmoor

Cavaliero, Glen, 'Reversions to Type', in *The Supernatural and English Fiction: From 'The Castle of Otranto' to 'Hawksmoor'* (Oxford: Oxford University Press, 1995), 224–8.

de Lange, Adrian, M., 'The Complex Architectonics of Postmodernist Fiction: *Hawksmoor* – A Case Study', in Theo D'haen and Hans Bertens (eds.), *British Postmodern Fiction*, Postmodern Studies 7 (Amsterdam and Atlanta: Rodopi, 1993), 145–65.

Herman, Luc, 'The Relevance of History: *Der Zauberbaum* (1985) by Peter Sloterdijk and *Hawksmoor* (1985) by Peter Ackroyd', in Theo D'haen and Hans Bertens (eds.), *History and Post-War Writing*, Postmodern Studies 3 (Amsterdam and Atlanta: Rodopi, 1990), 107–24.

Hollinghurst, Alan, 'In Hieroglyph and Shadow', *TLS*, 27 September 1985, p. 1049.

Keates, Jonathan, 'Creaking Floorboards', *Observer*, 22 September 1985, p. 27.

King, Francis, 'A Voice from the Past', *Spectator*, 28 September 1995, pp. 29–30.

Lewis, Peter, 'The Truth and Nothing Like the Truth: History and Fiction', *Stand Magazine*, vol. 27, no. 2 (1986), 38–44.

Oates, Joyce Carol, 'The Highest Passion Is Terrour', *New York Times Book Review*, January 1986, p. 3.

Onega, Susana, 'Pattern and Magic in *Hawksmoor*', *Atlantis*, vol. xii, no. 2 (November 1991), 31–43.

—— 'Empiricism and the "Scientia Umbrarum" in *Hawksmoor*', in Francisco Collado (ed.), *Science, Literature and Interpretation: Essays on Twentieth-Century Literature and Critical Theory* (Zaragoza: Servicio de Publicaciones de la Universidad de Zaragoza, 1991), 117–38.

Reverand II, Cedrid D., 'Review of Peter Ackroyd's *Hawksmoor*',

Eighteenth Century Life, vol. 11, no. 2 (1987), 102–9.

Rogers, Pat, 'Street Wise', *London Review of Books*, 3 October 1985, pp. 18–19.

Rykwert, Joseph, *'Hawksmoor'*, *Art in America*, July 1986, pp. 11, 13.

Chatterton

Costa, Dominique, '*Chatterton*: An Analysis of Peter Ackroyd's Fictional World', *Actas do XVI Encontro da A.P.E.A.A.* (Vila Real: Universidade de Trás-os Montes e Alto Douro, March 1995), 317–26.

Dodsworth, Martin, 'Peter Ackroyd. *Chatterton'*, *TLS*, 11–17 September 1987, p. 976.

Donoghue, Denis, 'One Life Was Not Enough', *New York Times Book Review*, 17 January 1988, pp. 1, 40.

Finney, Brian, 'Peter Ackroyd: Postmodernist Play and *Chatterton'*, *Twentieth Century Literature*, vol. 38, no. 2 (summer 1992), 240–61.

González Abalos, Susana, 'The Metafictional Element in *Chatterton'* (University of Zaragoza MA dissertation, 1996).

Goodman, Walter, 'Books of the Times: *Chatterton'*, *New York Times*, 31 December 1987, p. LC23.

Hotho-Jackson, Sabine, 'Literary History in Literature: An Aspect of the Contemporary Novel', *Modern Sprak*, vol. lxxxvi, no. 2 (1992), 113–19.

Lodge, David, 'The Marvellous Boy', *New York Review of Books*, vol. 35, no. 6 (14 April 1988), 15–16.

Miller, Nolan, '*Chatterton'*, *Antioch Review*, vol. 46, no. 2 (1988), 267–8.

Monnickendam, Andrew, 'Peter Ackroyd: *Chatterton'*, *Anuari d'anglès*, vol. xi-xii (1990), 107.

Neve, Michael, 'The Living Dead', *History Today*, 38 (January 1988), 53–4.

Rabaté, Jean-Michel, 'À la recherche de Chatterton', *Quinzaine littéraire*, 1988, pp. 517–18.

First Light

Abel, Claude, 'Quarterly Fiction Review', *Contemporary Review. Literary Supplement*, 255 (1989), 45–8.

Cowley, John, 'Something Vengeful and Ancient', *New York Times Book Review*, 94 (1989), 15–16.

Glazebrook, Phillip, 'Watching What Makes Us Tick', *Spectator*, 22 April 1989, pp. 27–8.

Pritchard, William, 'London Forms: *First Light*, by Peter Ackroyd', *New Republic*, 4 September 1989, p. 39.

Rawson, Claude, 'Peter Ackroyd: *First Light'*, *TLS*, 24 April–4 May 1989, p. 453.

Wood, Michael, 'Looking Away', *London Review of Books*, vol. ii, no. 10 (18 May 1989), 19.

English Music

Barrell, John, 'Make the Music Mute', *London Review of Books*, 9 July 1992, pp. 7–8.

Buchan, James, 'The Relics of Learning', *Spectator*, 30 May 1992, pp. 24–5.

Clements, Denney, 'We're Poorer For Not Knowing that Art and Life Intertwine', *Wichita Eagle*, 28 February 1993, p. 4F.

Cook, Bruce, 'Double Dose of Tradition in Works by Peter Ackroyd', *Daily News of Los Angeles*, 25 October 1992, p. L12.

Diekmann, Katherine, '*English Music*, by Peter Ackroyd', *Village Voice Literary Supplement*, 8 December 1992, p. 6.

Dyer, Richard, 'Ackroyd's Inventive *English Music*', *Boston Globe*, 9 December 1992, p. 51.

Goodrich, Chris, 'Shadow Play', *Los Angeles Times*, 25 October 1992, p. 3.

Heyward, Michael, 'Tradition and a Highly Individual Talent', *Washington Post*, 18 October 1992, p. X07.

—— 'This "Music" is Out of Tune', *Rocky Mountain News*, 29 November 1992, p. 115.

Kemp, John, 'Prodigiously Clever, Of Course', *Literary Review*, May 1992, pp. 36–8.

Kemp, Peter, 'The Big Snooze', *Sunday Times*, 24 May 1992, p. 5.

Klinkenborg, Verlyn, 'Peter Ackroyd's Music', *New Yorker*, 23 November 1992, pp. 142–4.

Lehmann-Haupt, Christopher, 'An Entertainment for the Literary', *New York Times*, 9 November 1992, p. LC13.

Levenson, Michael, 'Tradition and the National Talent', *New Republic*, 18 January 1993, pp. 29–32.

Lurie, Alison, 'Hanging Out with Hogarth', *New York Times Book Review*, 11 October 1992, p. 7.

Mallon, Peter, 'A Music With Too Many Notes', *USA Today*, 27 November 1992, p. 05D.

Mallon, Thomas, 'Author's Latest Celebration of English Literature Needs a Bit More Spontaneity', *Houston Post*, 13 December 1992.

Matros, Michael, 'Sing a Song of England's Culture: Dreamy Visits by Old Masters Threaten to Drown out Story', *Columbus Dispatch*, 1 November 1992, p. 06C.

McAleer, John, 'Peter Ackroyd Hymns: "The Forms of Eternity"', *Chicago Tribune*, 1 November 1992, p. 6.

Mead, Rebecca, 'Talking with Peter Ackroyd the Music of Time', *Newsday*, 18 October 1992, p. 38.

Phillips, Alice H. G., 'Dreams, Literary Conceits Collide in Artistic Pastiche', *Philadelphia Inquirer*, 15 November 1992, p. F01.

Rifkind, Donna, 'Clever Mimicry Just Impersonates Genius', *Washington Times*, 4 October 1992, p. B8.

Robinson, Peter, 'Literary Fantasy in an English Boy's World', *San Francisco Chronicle*, 10 January 1993, p. 9.

Shippey, T. A., 'From the National Pool', *TLS*, 22 May 1992, p. 29.

Smardz, Zofia, 'English Music Celebrates England and Its Arts', *Baltimore Morning Sun*, 22 November 1992, p. 6H.

Voves, Ed., 'A Boy's Very Strange Search for Identity', *Philadelphia Daily News*, 6 October 1992, p. 35.

Walsh, John, 'Confessions of a Monopolylinguist', *Sunday Times*, 17 May 1992, section 6, pp. 4–5.

Wheeler, Edward T., 'Off Key', *Commonweal*, 26 March 1993, p. 25.

Wolfe, Peter, 'Scholarly Dreams: An Exploration into an English Imagination', *St Louis Post Dispatch*, 7 February 1993, p. 05F.

The House of Doctor Dee

Boland, Eavan, 'Confidence Tricked', *Observer*, 29 August 1993, p. 51.

Cumming, Laura, 'Exploring the Alchemy of Time', *Guardian Weekly*, 12 September 1993, p. 28.

Glover, Michael, 'Can't Get No Satisfaction', *Books*, September 1993, p. 8.

King, Francis, 'The Older the Better', *Spectator*, 11 September 1993, p. 27.

Korn, Eric, 'Evil in EC1', *TLS*, 10 September 1993, p. 20.

O'Regan, Gerard, 'Ackroyd Keeps the Veil Drawn', *Irish Independent*, 3 September 1994, pp. 8–9.

Dan Leno and the Limehouse Golem

Battersby, Eileen, 'Maybe It's Because He's a Londoner', *Irish Times*, 20 August 1994, p. 9.

Birmingham, Stephen, 'History and Fiction Blur in Victorian Murder Tale', *Washington Times*, 14 May 1995, p. B7.

Hughes-Hallett, Lucy, 'Relishing the Disgusting', *Sunday Times*, 18 September 1994, p. 12.

Keating, Peter, 'Here We Are Again!' *TLS*, 9 September 1994, p. 21.

Martin, Valerie, 'A Victorian Nightmare', *New York Times Book Review*, 16 April 1995, p. 7.

Sexton, David, 'Thereby Hangs a Tale', *Spectator*, 10 September 1994, p. 33.

Sinclair, Iain, 'The Cadaver Club', *London Review of Books*, 22 December 1994, pp. 20–2.

Talese, Nan A., 'A Death in London: But Was It Murder?', *Newsday*, 2 May 1995, p. B02.

Milton in America

Barnacle, Hugo, 'Let's not be puritanical', *Sunday Times*, 25 August 1996, p. 8.

Bayley, John, 'Even old Ocean smiled upon him', *The Times*, 29 August 1996, p. 37.

Grove, Valerie, 'How I Lost my Fear of Dying', *The Times*, 23 August 1996, p. 19.

Levi, Peter, 'Is this the region, this the soil, the clime?' *Spectator*, 7 September 1996, p. 34.

Miller, Karl, 'What if Milton had sailed away to become a stranger in paradise?' *Observer Review*, 1 September 1996, p. 16.

On the Biographies and other Nonfictional Works
PEN New Fiction I

Casserley, Mark, *PEN New Fiction I*, *TLS*, 30 November 1984, p. 1391.

Dickens

Allen, Bruce, '*Dickens*: A Crowded Old Curiosity Shop', *USA Today*, 21 March 1991, p. 06D.

Bergonzi, Bernard, 'Exploring the Heart of Artistic Creation', *Tablet*, 8 September 1990, p. 1130.

Bering-Jensen, Helle, 'A Biography about Dickens that Raises and Fulfills Great Expectations', *Washington Times*, 11 February 1991, p. F1.

Burgess, Anthony, 'The Master of All Hearts in a Dissolute Age', *Independent*, 9 September 1990, p. 19.

Busch, Frederick, 'The Best of Dickens', *Los Angeles Times*, 20 January 1991, p. 1.

Byatt, A. S., 'Dynamism of Age Fuelled Dickens' Work: *Dickens* by Peter Ackroyd', *Rocky Mountain News*, 3 March 1991, p. 20M.

Carey, John, 'Paper Tyger', *Sunday Times*, 2 September 1990, section 8.

D. S., 'Nota Bene', *TLS*, 27 August 1993, p. 16.

Edmiston, John, 'Tales of Two Writers Bring Them to Life', *The Houston Post*, 16 February 1992, p. C5.

Gill, Stephen, 'The Key to a Continent', *TLS*, 31 August–6 September 1990, pp. 911–12.

Hunter, Jefferson, 'In Dickens' Style, a Look at Dickens', *Philadelphia Inquirer*, 17 March 1991, p. F03.

Kaplan, Fred, 'Life Is Long and Full of Surprises', *Independent on Sunday*, 2 September 1990, p. 22.

Kincaid, James R., 'The Sun of his Oddities', *New York Book Review*, 13 January 1990, pp. 1, 24.

Klinkenborg, Verlyn, 'Book Reviews', *Smithsonian*, 23 (January 1993), 131–2.

Kogan, Bernard, 'Prodigious Dickens', *Chicago Tribune*, 20 January 1991, p. 3.

Lannon, Linnea, 'Biography of Dickens Tests Reader's Stamina', *Detroit Free Press*, 20 January 1991, p. 8G.

Marcus, Stephen, 'Dickens on an Epic Scale', *Newsday*, 10 February 1991, p. 25.

Maves, Carl, 'The Duality of Dickens', *San Francisco Chronicle*, 27 January 1991, p. 1.

Porter, Roy, 'Boz's Great Expectations', *Evening Standard*, 30 August 1990, p. 29.

Raine, Craig, 'Odds and Ends of a Great Life', *Observer*, 2 September 1990, p. 63.

Rivière, William, 'Dickens' Definition of Moral Order', *Catholic Herald*, 14 September 1990, p. 6.

Rubin, Merle, 'Revisiting Dickens (and Friend)', *Christian Society Monitor*, 25 February 1991, p. 13.

Sharper, Diane, 'Ackroyd Biography Depicts Charles Dickens' Lifelong Search for a Muse', *Baltimore Morning Sun*, 10 February 1991, p. 6C.

Short, Shirley, 'An In-Depth Examination of the Life of One of Britain's Premier Novelists', *Kentucky Post*, 26 December 1991, p. 4K.

Spurling, Hilary, 'From a Bridge of Tears', *Weekend Telegraph*, 8 September 1990, p. xii.

Starr, William, 'Writer Captures Dickens' Genius', *The State*, 3 February 1991, p. 5F.

Sutherland, John, 'A Terrible Bad Cold', *London Review of Books*, vol. 12, no. 18 (27 September 1990), 17–18.

Walker, Ruth, 'Dickens: A Matter of Relentless Research', *Virginian Pilot*, 10 February 1991, p. C2.

Introduction to Dickens
Ray, Kevin, 'Introducing Mr. Dickens', *St Louis Post Dispatch*, 26 July 1992, p. 5C.

Dickens' London: An Imaginative Vision
Sanders, Andrew, 'Review of *Dickens' London: An Imaginative Vision*', *Dickensian*, vol. 84, no. 415 (1988), 110–12.

Blake
Bull, Malcolm, 'Liberty Boy–Genius', *TLS*, 20 October 1995, p. 3–4.

The Life of Thomas More
Carey, John, 'The Life of Thomas More by Peter Ackroyd', *Sunday Times*, 22 February 1998, pp. 1–2.

Colinson, Patrick, 'Defined by his death', *TLS*, 13 March 1998, pp. 3–4.

Stanford, Peter, 'Church of Past Times', *Independent on Sunday*, 1 March 1998, pp. 26–7.

Thomas, Keith, 'Utopia and Beyond', *The Guardian*, 12 March 1998, p. 14.

Index